THE ACCIDENTAL

MEDICAL WRITER

How We Became Successful

Freelance Medical Writers.

How You Can, Too.

THE ACCIDENTAL

MEDICAL WRITER

How We Became Successful
Freelance Medical Writers.
How You Can, Too.

By

Cynthia L. Kryder, MS, CCC-Sp

and

Brian G. Bass

DEDICATION

To my family: husband Kim, and daughters Chelsea and Shannon. You motivate me to do my very best always. Thank you for your support and love.

Cyndy Kryder
August 2008

For my wife, Andrea, and my daughters, Morgan and Courtney, whose encouragement makes my success possible and whose love makes it meaningful.

Brian Bass
August 2008

Table of Contents

http://www.theaccidentalmedicalwriter.com

About the Authors

Cyndy Kryder has worked in the field of health care in some way ever since she grabbed her Master's Degree in 1977 and headed to her first professional job as a speech-language pathologist at a private school in suburban Philadelphia. Her 9-year stint working in a pediatric-rehabilitation hospital developed her passion for writing patient-education materials and cemented her interest in the field of medicine. She launched her freelance medical writing career in 1992 and is thankful for the freedom and flexibility it offers her. Like her coauthor, Brian Bass, Cyndy currently writes promotional, educational, and scientific pieces for professionals and lay audiences in a number of different therapeutic areas and for a wide range of media. She also assists companies in their publication-planning efforts. A member of the Delaware Valley Chapter of the American Medical Writers Association (AMWA), Cyndy presents workshops and leads roundtable discussions on various topics for freelance medical writers and editors.

http://www.theaccidentalmedicalwriter.com

Brian Bass has been a professional writer for all of his career, including more than 20 years experience as a freelance medical writer specializing in medical education, communications, and advertising. He went out on his own in 1989 and never looked back. Today, Brian writes scientific, educational, and promotional materials for health care professional and lay audiences in a wide range of therapeutic areas for print, electronic, and interactive media. He has won awards for his work in sales training, sales motivation, and physician education. His successful freelance medical writing business now includes a team of other highly qualified freelance medical writers who work with him, including his coauthor, Cyndy Kryder. Brian is a member of the American Medical Writers Association (AMWA), and he frequently presents workshops, roundtables, and panel discussions on topics of interest to freelance writers and editors at local and national meetings in the United States and abroad.

You can contact Cyndy and Brian at http://www.theaccidentalmedicalwriter.com.

This book provides you with the benefits of almost 40 years of collective freelance medical writing experience, consolidated into these lessons, mistakes, and tips. Keep reading to learn more.

Cyndy's Lessons:

Lesson #1: It doesn't matter if you don't have so-called "published" pieces. Most people can find something they've written to include in their portfolio.

Lesson #2: Always, always, always get paid to learn something new.

Lesson #3: You have to spend money to make money.

Cyndy's Mistakes:

Mistake #1: Being seduced by the allure of a regular paycheck.

Mistake #2: Treating freelancing like a job, not a business.

Mistake #3: Trying to do it all.

Mistake #4: Marketing to the wrong audience.

Cyndy's Tips:

Tip #1: Find mentors who know what they're doing and listen to their advice.

Tip #2: Join the American Medical Writers Association.

Tip #3: Buy the right desktop resources.

Tip #4: Become proficient with your computer software.

Tip #5: Update your software regularly.

Tip #6: Always say yes.

Tip #7: Market yourself continually.

Tip #8: Honor your deadlines.

Brian's Lessons:

Lesson #1: It doesn't matter what you know. What matters is what you learn, and what people are willing to teach you.

Lesson #2: It is easier to get forgiveness than it is to get permission.

Lesson #3: With good input and direction, plus a good example or two, you can do almost anything.

Lesson #4: Never underestimate the motivating power of fear.

Lesson #5: If you want good people to work for you, pay them well and pay them on time.

Lesson #6: Relevance is relative.

Lesson #7: Every time the phone rings, it's a chance to be a hero.

Lesson #8: The time to look for work is NOT when you need it.

Lesson #9: If you want to win the race, you've got to cross the finish line.

Lesson #10: Never stop taking risks.

Brian's Mistakes:

Mistake #1: Not knowing what I couldn't do.

Mistake #2: Not trusting my instincts.

Brian's Tips:

Tip #1: Know what you know, and know what you don't know.

Tip #2: Promise what you will deliver, and deliver on what you promise.

Tip #3: Deliver on time, on target, and on budget; first time and every time.

http://www.theaccidentalmedicalwriter.com

Introduction

We both started out unqualified to do what we do today for a living. We came to the same career from very different experiences, educations, expectations, and needs. Today, we are both successful freelance medical writers.

Cyndy was a health care professional who never planned on becoming a writer. Brian was a writer who never planned on entering the health care profession. Cyndy grew up at the end of an era where women were relegated to certain roles and career choices and rarely switched boats in midstream. Brian grew up at the end of the same era, when a man was expected to get a good job and stick with it until retirement.

We wrote this book for everyone who is frustrated with working for someone else. For everyone who wants the freedom and security that freelance medical writing can help them achieve. We wrote this book to tell you how we became successful, so you can gain the confidence and skills to become successful, too.

In our journeys to becoming successful freelance medical writers, we made different mistakes and learned different lessons. The tips we have to share with you can help you avoid some of the pitfalls and perhaps get to the benefits that freelance medical writing has to offer a bit faster.

We have worked together as colleagues for a long time, and we are committed to sharing what we know with other professionals who are interested in pursuing freelance medical writing as a career. Over the years, we found that giving seminars at local and national meetings was one way to reach aspiring freelance medical writers, but it never felt like quite enough. That's why we wrote this book, launched a website, and made a commitment to publish an entire series of books to help you achieve your personal and professional goals.

When we started out, we often found ourselves flying by the seats of our pants. We did things intuitively because 20 years ago there wasn't a lot of information out there about how to become a medical writer, let alone how to become a *freelance* medical writer. As you will find when you read our stories, it wasn't always easy.

It is our hope that by reading about our unqualifications and our quests for success, you will be inspired and armed to take a risk and pursue something for which you, too, might feel that you are currently unqualified. That doesn't mean that anyone can become a successful freelance medical writer. You can't go from plumbing, for example, to medical writing, without some type of commensurate experience, either in science, writing, health care, or a similar area of expertise. Medical writing requires a distinct set of skills, which you will be able to discern as you read this book and others in our series. A medical or science background helps, but isn't essential. Likewise, a writing background can provide an advantage, but isn't mandatory.

Is this book just for people who want to become successful freelance medical writers? No. The strategies, lessons, and tips that we provide can be applied to any freelance endeavor. We achieved our success through medical writing, but our tips and techniques can be applied to other types of writing as well as to other types of freelance businesses.

Is this book just for people who are in the same circumstances in which we found ourselves at the time we first became freelance medical writers? No again. Freelance medical writing is a perfect career choice whether you're returning to the workforce or planning your exit, plotting a career change, or releasing your inner muse.

This book will give you the confidence you need to get started and the foundation you need to become successful. The other books in our series will teach you how to do what we do, so you can overcome your personal unqualifications and become a successful freelance medical writer, too.

Will this book make you a successful freelance writer by itself? No. But with its tips, strategies, and lessons, it holds the potential to give you a foundation on which to build your own success, however you define that for yourself. You ultimately are the one who determines your success. You'll decide which messages in this book to take to heart and which to discard. Your success lies within you.

Are you ready to take the next step?

Section 1: Cyndy's Story

My Unqualifications

I had my initial clue that my career wasn't going to mesh well with my lifestyle as a parent when my female boss called me 4 hours after I delivered our first child and requested a teleconference to discuss certain work-related issues that just couldn't wait. I had gone into labor around midnight, delivered our daughter at 5:45 that Monday morning, and by 9 a.m. all I wanted to do was breathe in the beauty of my newborn and possibly take a well-deserved nap. In the euphoric haze that accompanies childbirth, there was no way I could lead a conference call and sound intelligent on the phone.

At that point in my life my official job title was Clinical Director at a suburban Philadelphia rehabilitation hospital. In that capacity, I managed a residential-living program that retrained adults with traumatic brain injury and taught them how to live independently. I directed staff, managed budgets, soothed the frayed nerves of patients and their families, and was the person responsible when something went wrong. And if you know anything about health care, you know that things always go wrong.

Still, I enjoyed my job and was perfectly willing to put in the extra hours necessary to get everything done. My salary was adequate (not great), benefits were good (OK, looking back, those were definitely great), and, having been recently promoted, I felt as though I was climbing the corporate health care ladder. With a master's degree in speech/language pathology from Bloomsburg State College (now Bloomsburg University) in Pennsylvania, plus 12 years of experience working as a speech pathologist under my belt, moving into an administrative position was exactly what I wanted to do.

7

As one of those women who came of age during women's liberation, I had always assumed that I could have it all—and have it all at the same time. But I never considered myself to be driven. I worked hard to maintain a balance between work and play and enjoyed satisfying activities outside of work: gardening, sewing, and reading, to name a few. Being bulldozed by an aggressive boss who placed work before family was never part of the plan.

The morning I became a parent I kindly declined to participate in the conference call and took that nap instead, but I spent the next 2 years juggling my professional work and my personal life. Parenting was tougher and more enjoyable than I had ever imagined. With the birth of our second child, and a paycheck that was dwindling as more dollars went to pay for day care, I knew I needed to do something else.

With an infant on my lap and a toddler dancing around the kitchen, I called my neighbor, a 50-something successful medical writer, and asked the question that opened the door to my career in freelance medical writing: "Tell me how I can write stuff and get paid for it."

****

Why have I told you all of this? Well, I'm certainly not trying to reinforce the assumption that it's not what you know but who you know, although having a mentor to nurture you along the way is something I would recommend (you'll read more about that later). Nor is this meant to be an endorsement of working motherhood.

What I'm trying to demonstrate here–and my colleague, Brian, is trying to convey as well—is the circuitous paths we took to medical writing. And if we could do it, so can you.

8

When I graduated from college with an advanced degree in speech pathology, I didn't even know what a medical writer was. Today I'm the sole proprietor of a successful freelance medical writing business who's produced materials for some of the major pharmaceutical players: Abbott, Wyeth, Bristol-Myers Squibb, Johnson & Johnson, Novartis, and Pfizer. I've been a medical writer for more than 16 years now, and I don't see an end in sight, although God may have other plans.

Convincing folks that a speech pathologist could become a writer—and a good one at that—was a challenge. Even my husband, Kim, scoffed when I told him I was going to earn a living as a freelance medical writer. "A writer?" he asked. "What kind of experience do YOU have as a writer?"

Good point.

I'd like to tell you that the whole business of, well, developing a business was easy, but I won't lie to you. Work and money didn't just flow automatically once I hung out my freelance shingle. There were some years when my receivables were well under the poverty level and others when I billed out enough to feel confident about paying 2 college tuitions in the future. One year, days stretched into weeks that stretched into months without a paying job coming across my desk. It was tough and disheartening—and I began to panic. I knew what my husband was thinking, even though it was unspoken: "At least do something to bring in some bucks, because my salary isn't enough to support all of our needs." But I never gave up, despite the bumps and bruises I encountered along the way. And I know you can benefit from my experience.

You're obviously interested in learning more about how to become a medical writer or you wouldn't have bothered to buy this book. So let me warn you up front. In these pages you won't find a step-by-step plan that you should follow exactly to become a successful freelance medical writer. Instead, you'll read about how Brian and I developed careers in a field where some of our potential clients (and former colleagues from our previous professional lives) considered us unqualified. We'll tell you the things we did right, but, more importantly, we'll explain where we went wrong; you'll have the benefit of hindsight. Along the way, you'll find practical advice that you can use to make changes in your own life.

As you read this book, you'll see that Brian and I took quite different paths, but ended up in similar places. He had more experience in writing, advertising, and marketing; I had more experience in health care and a background as a clinician. Both of us had the entrepreneurial drive to work independently and create our own businesses. Neither of us is a doctor or a nurse or an English major. For better or worse, our strengths and weaknesses dictated the choices we made when we took the leap into freelance medical writing.

The fact that the wage I earned was secondary income for my family also played a major role in the business decisions I made (or avoided, for that matter). With a husband who worked full time and brought home the benefits, I had the luxury to grow my business more slowly than did Brian. And being a female affected the approach I took to my freelance career. Yes, as much as I hate to admit this even though it's true, gender does make a difference, as you'll see when you compare Brian's story with mine.

If freelance medical writing is something you're considering, but you don't feel qualified, don't be discouraged. You can make it big in the business of freelance medical writing without experience. I know. I did it. So did my coauthor. And so can you.

Lessons Learned

My neighbor, Donna, gave me some good advice that winter morning. She put me in touch with Wini who, at that time, was developing her own start-up business and needed freelance writers who could review and analyze clinical evidence to determine whether a medical procedure, drug, or device was safe and efficacious. I called her up, expressed my interest in writing for her, scheduled an interview, arranged for a babysitter, and started biting my nails when I realized that she expected to see my portfolio.

Portfolio? What in the world had I written that I could put into a portfolio? Nothing published, that's for sure. Or at least that's what I thought.

Contrary to what my husband believed about my lack of writing experience, I did have a few writing samples I could share. I had written a chapter about language and learning disorders that appeared in a published college textbook. My name appeared as a coauthor of a journal manuscript that had been recently published. And there was that article I wrote in our hospital's glossy marketing magazine that talked about the multiple sclerosis program I managed.

Hmmm. Could I count those letters to the editor I sent years ago to a few local newspapers commenting on Pennsylvania's proposed seat belt law? Why not? And let's not forget those handouts I created when I was a speech therapist to help the families of the patients I treated understand their children's disorders. Bingo! I had my portfolio and I learned a valuable lesson:

11

LESSON #1:

It doesn't matter if you don't have so-called "published" pieces. Most people can find something they've written to include in their portfolio.

Not only did I have my portfolio, but it was a balanced one at that. If I put the right spin on things, I could show prospective clients that I could write for multiple audiences, including students and educators (college textbook), professionals (journal manuscript), everyday people (glossy magazine article and letters to the editor), and patients and their families (my therapy handouts).

Being able to write for different audiences is an important skill you want to acquire if you're planning to work in this business. Writing for only one type of audience pigeonholes you and leaves you vulnerable when there's a downturn in that particular sector of the industry. Having the skill to write for multiple audiences not only makes you more appealing to future customers (and gives you a broader customer base), it gives you more flexibility in choosing projects. If you're like me, you want some variety in your projects. There are few people I know who want to get stuck working on the same kinds of projects week after week, year after year.

The day of my meeting with Wini I dressed in my interview suit, free of baby formula, packed my samples into my briefcase, and turned on my professional charm. (Yes, even though I was vying for a freelance position and would be working out of my solitary home office, I still needed to look and act professional. Contrary to what you might think, being a freelance isn't always about writing in your bunny slippers.) I was concerned, though, that my portfolio wouldn't be relevant enough, particularly since none of my writing samples came close to resembling

12

a technology assessment, the kind of writing Wini was expecting from me. Heck, when I walked into that interview, I wasn't even clear about what a technology assessment was!

Much to my surprise, Wini was impressed with my portfolio, one that I had thought was simply "good enough." (As my coauthor, Brian, explains, relevance is relative.) She was intrigued with my experience in head injury rehabilitation, especially since she recently had been contracted by a client to evaluate the effectiveness of a certain form of head injury rehabilitation, which just happened to be my specialty. She hired me on the spot as a freelance writer to produce my first report for her company, one of many I would end up writing for her.

Lucky break, you say? I'd have to disagree. I see it as 2 lucky breaks. First, I had a neighbor who was a medical writer and then I found a businesswoman looking for someone with exactly my kind of experience. How often does that happen? If I needed a sign that I was meant to begin my writing career, then I certainly had it.

It took me multiple hours to write that first report, I don't even remember how many anymore. I do know that I spent more hours writing it than I was paid for. Why? Because Wini was a smart business owner. Given that this was all new to me, and she and I both knew I would have a significant learning curve, we agreed up front to an hourly rate ($25) and a maximum number of hours (40) for writing the report.

Was I stupid or desperate to agree to such an arrangement? Neither. As a matter of fact I was being quite smart. And this leads me to the next lesson:

LESSON #2:

Always, always, always get paid to learn something new.

Sure, I knew a lot about rehabilitation and health care, and I knew how to write a decent research paper. After all, I had written a graduate thesis. What I wasn't familiar with were the styles and conventions routinely used in medical writing. As I saw it, this arrangement would be a win-win situation. I would be paid $1000 to learn how to write (in other professions it's called on-the-job training) and Wini would end up with a document she would later sell to her clients. If Wini was satisfied with the report, and with me and my ability, I knew she'd give me additional projects, and repeat business was something else I was looking for. Remember, keeping a customer is easier than attracting new ones.

Yes, I know that if I were writing that same report today I'd charge a lot more money. But I have years of experience now, which I didn't have then. Plus I'm a better writer. When I got started in this business, I had no false expectations that I could command top dollar for my work, and neither should you. But I certainly didn't believe then, and I don't believe now (nor does my coauthor), that any writer, no matter what their specialty, should write something for free, just to get some experience, which leads me to another lesson:

LESSON #3:

You have to spend money to make money.

If this sounds contrary to Lesson #2, let me explain. When I accepted Wini's writing assignment, she was paying me to learn something new, but I was also spending money in the hopes of ultimately making more money. The money I spent was in the form of the additional unpaid hours I accrued while preparing the report. Those extra hours were my investment in my new career, and one that has paid off handsomely—in experience, repeat business, and dollars in my bank account, as well as connections in the medical writing world. I never regretted agreeing to that financial arrangement, even though some readers might not consider it ideal, because it put my foot in the door and the door didn't slap me on the behind.

So, was that first report a great document? It was adequate. Fortunately, Donna offered to edit my initial drafts for free and to sit down with me and explain some basic medical writing rules (remember my earlier comment about mentors?). With her advice, I avoided a few of the common writing mistakes that would have made my writing appear quite amateur.

Still, Wini was satisfied and so was her client. I had learned some basics about medical writing, I received a hefty check to cash, and, most importantly, I had additional work from Wini, who was happy indeed to add another writer to her stable. And guess what? Wini paid me $30 an hour for the next report, a rate increase of 20%! Not too bad for a speech therapist with, according to my hubby and some former colleagues, limited writing experience.

Basking in the satisfaction of a job well done, I was on my way to having it all. Or so I thought.

You Can Learn From My Mistakes

This would be a great story if I could tell you that Wini was just one of many clients I worked for during my first year as a freelance medical writer; that I billed out six figures in receivables that first year alone; that I was happy and satisfied with the balance between work and family. But it's not true, mostly because I made a lot of mistakes when I started out.

Since I had been so successful at my first foray into medical writing, I failed to look at this new career path truly as a business and, instead, considered it a part-time job. Wini, needing freelance writers who would be available to work for her as needed, was eager to guarantee me a set number of hours each week, whatever I could provide her, within reason. Given that my 2 young children were the primary reason I had switched careers, I wasn't looking to work more than 20 hours a week, and Wini was satisfied with this arrangement. So was I, which led me to my first big mistake:

MISTAKE #1:
Being seduced by the allure of a regular paycheck.

In my eagerness to once again be contributing to the family coffer on a regular basis, I became seduced by the comfort of a monthly paycheck. Twenty hours a week meant working 4 hours a day Monday through Friday. By working those 20 hours a week, I received a check for roughly $2400 each month. Woo-hoo! At the end of the year, it would add up to about $30,000, less than what I had been making before, but an adequate sum considering that I was only working part time.

What I didn't take into consideration was that by guaranteeing one client 20 hours a week, I was already limiting the number of other clients for whom I could work, as well as the amount of money I could make and the other medical writing skills I could learn.

Unfortunately, the security of a regular paycheck can be overwhelming. I know because it was for me. Although I was anxious to have more flexibility with my work schedule and I wanted to work for myself, I wasn't ready for the uncertainty that accompanies any form of freelance writing. Let's face it. Freelancing is messy. You have to market yourself and your abilities constantly, you have to dig around for work, and then you have to wait for who knows how long to be paid. You might expect your clients to pay you within 30 days, but in reality that rarely happens. In my experience, it's more common to wait 60 or even 90 days after billing for your clients to pay up.

I have to admit, too, that I'm impatient. At that point in my life, I had an emotional need (and a financial one) to be earning my own money, and to earn it RIGHT NOW. I didn't want to wait months to receive a check for work I had performed months before. I wanted that immediate satisfaction, and so I chose to work for one client for 20 hours a week, all the hours I wanted to devote, at that time, to work. And that led to another big mistake:

MISTAKE #2:

Treating freelancing like a job, not a business.

After a few months, working for Wini became very comfortable. I had become familiar with the format of the reports I was writing, learned how to use the word-processing program, and discovered that I was quite good at performing database searches. It was challenging because every day I was learning about new medical technologies, and learning new skills had always been a criterion for any job I took. Eventually I even moved into the position of managing editor, still on a freelance basis. But this was nothing more than another employee-employer relationship. I was working for one client, producing one type of document. Sure, I had a home office and business deductions for the IRS, but I certainly couldn't call it a thriving business, even though I was usually working more than 20 hours a week.

In my excitement of finding someone who would pay me to write stuff, I had failed to put together even a rudimentary business plan. I never gave a thought to branding, or marketing, or advertising, nor did I consult an accountant or attorney to discuss the advantages of a sole proprietorship versus becoming a corporation. You might say that I took the *"Ready, Fire, Aim"* approach to starting my business, not something I would recommend. In my haste to begin writing, I rushed into an arrangement that, although satisfactory, was not really moving me toward what I thought was my ultimate goal: a freelance medical writing business of my own. I limited myself from the very beginning by making those choices.

What I should have done, and what I'm advising you to do, was to learn all I could about the medical writing business before taking on that first client. I needed to find out as much as I could about the scope of medical writing, who hired medical writers, and the different types of documents medical writers produced so that I could determine what would be a good fit for me. (You can learn more about the scope of medical writing in a future book in our series.) I should have, at the very least, formulated some initial, concrete business goals and a plan for achieving those goals. ("Having my own writing business" isn't really a concrete goal.) And I should have learned a little something about marketing and promotion so that I could market myself to other agencies that hired medical writers instead of putting all of my eggs into one basket, so to speak.

With Donna's encouragement, I joined the American Medical Writers Association (AMWA) during my first year of freelancing (you'll read more about this organization in later sections). AMWA was a wonderful resource, and the regional meetings were an excellent opportunity to connect with other writers and learn about aspects of the medical writing business. But it didn't fill all my needs.

What I wanted desperately back then was a book that would explain to me what a drug monograph was, and a detail aid, and a backgrounder, and a sales-training script. I needed a resource that told me exactly how to write a journal manuscript and how to pull together an abstract. Because I couldn't find one, I stumbled through as best I could.

Was the result all bad? You can probably guess the answer. Of course it wasn't. Think back to Lesson #2: *Always, always, always get paid to learn something new.* I was getting paid to soak up everything I could about medical writing in this venue. Donna was acting as my mentor and, with the periodic inservices Wini required the writers to attend, I was learning quite a bit about writing in general and medical writing in particular, as well as other topics that would come in handy, including

20

basic statistics, the pharmaceutical industry, and the US Food and Drug Administration (FDA) regulatory and drug-development processes.

Let's talk a bit about those inservices. Wini was unique in that she provided inservices for her writers. Agencies and individuals who hire medical writers rarely, if ever, do this. They expect the writers they hire to already have the knowledge they need to write effectively, or at least to know where to look on their own to get it. Wini, however, understood that the technology assessments her company produced were quite different from the materials medical writers usually create. And, frankly, Wini just couldn't find that many writers with statistical and technology-assessment experience who were interested in working for a start-up firm that wasn't able to pay their writers top dollar. So, in order for the freelance writers she hired to create accurate reports, she needed to train us in the very particular skills we needed so we could analyze clinical-trial information and report on a technology's efficacy and safety. It was a huge benefit to me as a beginning writer, and the knowledge I gained then still comes in handy today.

Fortunately for me, Wini recognized my management capabilities and soon promoted me to freelance managing editor. In my new position, I had daily (by telephone) interactions with the freelance writers who worked for us. I got to know them on a personal and professional level and, even better, I heard about the other clients for whom they worked. Through these connections, I built networks with other medical writers and other companies that hired freelance medical writers. A few of these companies offered me occasional freelance work, which I took even while I worked for Wini, since I was getting itchy to write something besides technology assessments. Plus I could charge more for these freelance assignments than I was earning as managing editor, so it made perfect sense to cultivate some additional freelance clients on the side. But I was also getting tired, because of my biggest mistake:

MISTAKE #3:

Trying to do it all.

When I agreed to work at least 20 hours a week, I had the irrational belief that I could do this without child care. In case you've forgotten, let me remind you that I had 2 children, now ages 6 months and 2 and a half years, as well as a husband, 3 dogs, 2 cats, and a 4-bedroom house on a half acre of land, with gardens that needed to be weeded and grass that needed to be mowed. My husband worked full time and attended evening meetings on an almost-weekly basis. I was the glue that held everything together and kept all the balls balanced in the air.

My plan was to try to write (and to schedule important work-related telephone conversations) during the day when the girls were napping. Since naps were never a sure thing, I frequently wrote at night after they went to bed, often from 9 p.m. until 1 or 2 in the morning. If you're a parent yourself, you know that infants and toddlers are early risers, so I was frequently getting up again at 7 a.m. to tend to the children. Unlike a certain well-known domestic diva with the initials M.S., I need more than 5 hours of sleep a night. Life was exhausting, but it didn't have to be.

Would a man have approached a part-time writing gig this way? I kind of doubt it. Being female and with those mothering genes working overtime, I mistakenly believed that what was best for my kids was to stay at home with their working mother as their primary caregiver. And this prohibited me from working as many hours as I could have to launch my new career and make it successful. Essentially, it limited my earning potential.

22

My coauthor, Brian, addresses an unfortunate reality in today's society, and that's the gender gap in the workplace and even among freelance writers. He correctly points out that one cause of this gap may be that women are less aware of their real value in the marketplace. I believe this is true, but I also think the gender gap is one result of the way we females are genetically wired. In my experience men seem better able to compartmentalize the various aspects of their lives and can make a clear distinction between the responsibilities at home and work. Women, on the other hand (or at least me), make less of a distinction. When we work, we think about what we need to do at home. When we're at home, we're thinking about what we need to do at work. It becomes a vicious cycle that, in my opinion, contributes to the gender gap.

I should have taken my own advice and learned Lesson #3: *You have to spend money to make money.* But at the time our budget was fragile, and I was reluctant to burden it with additional expenses for child care, even for a few hours a day. So I kept this schedule until my daughters entered nursery school, when I could write during the hours they were in school. The day they both entered elementary school was a benchmark day because I was finally able to write from 9 a.m. until 3 p.m. without interruption.

That year I took a hard look at my situation and clarified my goals. Wini's company had grown to the point where a managing editor was needed on a full-time basis, often on site. Plus Wini started asking me to accompany her on frequent business trips, and that required quite a bit of scheduling to arrange before- and after-school child care. Honestly, it wasn't something I was interested in doing right then because I still wanted to be able to do those "mom" things, like attending school plays and chaperoning field trips.

Wini and I both knew that for her business to grow to the next level, she needed a full-time managing editor. She offered me the position, but I declined. My instincts told me that it was time to move on.

It was a bittersweet decision, for both of us, when I chose to focus exclusively on the freelance side of my business. Depending on your attitude, giving up the security of a regular paycheck, even as a freelance, can be either freeing or frightening. I chose to make the experience a liberating one and put my panic on hold, although I did sweat quite a bit thinking about having to pay college tuition for 2 kids in a few years. I wholeheartedly agree with my coauthor when he states that fear is motivating!

Wini and I didn't end our relationship, though. I'm not one to burn bridges and neither is she. We remain good friends and colleagues to this day and I occasionally take on freelance projects for her company. Her business has grown dramatically, and I'm happy and satisfied with mine, so the decision for me to move on was a mutually beneficial one.

Having made the decision to focus exclusively on my freelance business, it was time for me to get busy. With the relationships I made while working for Wini and the networks I created through AMWA, I knew scores of people in the business. I called and emailed those companies I had freelanced for in the past and let them know I was available to take on more work. I thought I had a good idea of who else I could market myself to. And this leads me to the final whopper of a mistake I want to tell you about:

MISTAKE #4:

Marketing to the wrong audience.

Do you remember when I told you that I should have taken the time to learn more about the scope of medical writing and find out who hires freelance medical writers on a regular basis? I thought I knew who would hire me. Unfortunately, even though I had been in the business a few years and had made numerous contacts, I had a skewed view of the pharmaceutical and health care industries. You see, I had worked for one company that produced reports for the insurance market, plus I had freelanced for the occasional pharmaceutical client. Sure I had learned about other aspects of medical writing through my AMWA connections, but in my inexperience I wrongly assumed that hospitals and pharmaceutical companies would be my biggest clients.

Why was this assumption a mistake? Because hospitals and pharmaceutical companies generally enlist medical communications agencies and medical education companies (as preferred vendors) to meet their key communications or educational needs, and I had neglected to include such companies on my list of potential clients.

At this point you might be asking yourself what exactly are medical communications companies. These are agencies that work with manufacturers of pharmaceuticals, biologicals, and medical devices to provide services and develop creative products (think videos, CD-ROMS, slide decks, even flashy print materials) for multiple audiences that will communicate key messages about the drug or device they are selling. Generally these companies are full-service agencies; that is, they can do it all, from strategic planning to website development, to event planning and implementation, to manuscript development and placement in peer-reviewed medical journals. Because they offer such a variety of services, companies that specialize in medical communications have a great need for writers to keep up with the demands of their clients.

Medical education companies are similar full-service agencies, except they tend to focus exclusively on continuing medical education (CME). Health care professionals are required to obtain continuing-education credits on a regular basis by attending presentations on various topics. Medical education companies create these presentations in various media: live symposia, web-based programs, or targeted direct-mail CME-accredited newsletters, to name a few.

Go to your favorite search engine and type in "medical communications companies" or "medical education companies" and you'll find the names of both big and small players in the industry. These agencies, particularly the smaller ones, are always in the market for skilled and dependable freelance medical writers who can join their teams.

I wish I had known about these companies when I was starting out because it might have made a huge difference in the speed at which my business grew. But, if you recall, my background was in direct patient care; since I lacked what I consider to be vital knowledge of pharmaceutical marketing and advertising, these agencies didn't even appear on my personal radar.

Still, despite my big mistakes, each year I attracted more and more clients due, in large part, to my clinical background and my ability to write for patients and their families. My revenue increased steadily. So did my reputation as a talented writer. All because of the things I did right.

The Things I Did Right

Now that I've told you about some of my biggest mistakes, let me tell you about a few of the things I did right. Previously I told you how my neighbor, Donna, edited those initial drafts of the first-ever document I produced as a bona fide medical writer. Being an English major, Donna knew the intricacies of writing as only someone with a degree in English could. Plus she was ruthless with the red editing pencil. When I looked over my draft after she was finished with it, my heart began to flutter and I started to sweat. (In medical lingo, that's arrhythmia and diaphoresis.) The manuscript was bloody with red on every page.

At that point I could have become defensive and disregarded Donna's valuable suggestions, or I could accept Donna's mentoring and attempt to learn something from the experience. It was my choice. After taking a deep breath, I removed my heart (figuratively, of course), wrapped it in a box, and put it on the shelf, along with my ego. Although I thought my writing was brilliant (and, be honest, as writers don't we always think our writing is brilliant, at least initially?), obviously I was wrong. And this brings me to my first tip:

TIP #1:

Find mentors who know what they're doing and listen to their advice.

Notice that I didn't tell you simply to FIND a mentor. You might have the most talented writer in the world acting as your mentor, but if you aren't ready (or willing) to accept advice, the mentoring will be of no value.

Conversely, you could be a sponge, waiting to absorb as much information as possible, but if your mentor is not that knowledgeable or talented, you won't gain much from the experience.

I want to be completely honest with you. There are some freelance medical writers out there who are making a living, but they aren't very good. How do I know this? I've worked with some of them and I've edited the work of others.

If you have the skill to sell yourself and you know how to string words together to make sentences and sentences to make paragraphs, you can probably get hired in this industry. Notice that I put the selling yourself part before the writing part. Some of my colleagues might disagree with me on this point—and they're entitled to their opinions—but I've seen it happen. You might not get repeat work from your clients, but you'll likely get that initial job. Why?

People who know how to toot their own horns, even if they don't have much substance, can come across as being very impressive. In addition, unfortunate but true, some companies rely heavily on editors to correct all the writing mistakes that so-so writers make, enabling even mediocre writers to get hired. These companies have the philosophy that it's better to have medical knowledge and experience (and usually a degree to back that up) than writing skills. Other companies don't have the resources (and that includes time as well as money) for editors to review everything writers produce. Those companies expect the writing to be first rate beginning with the initial draft. In my opinion that's a perfectly reasonable expectation and one that I never wavered from when I was a managing editor.

Let me tell you this. As a managing editor, I looked for writers whose work did not require extensive editing. Think about it. The less editing that was necessary, the lower the company's cost to produce the document and the quicker I could get it to the client and invoice them for the service. It wasn't a complex formula.

The point here is not that I'm telling you to be judgmental, but that you have to be discerning. There is a difference. Who would you rather have as your mentor: the so-so writer whose drafts require extensive editing or the careful writer who pays close attention to details and sends in a nearly perfect first draft every time?

When you read Brian's story you'll see that he, too, found a great mentor, albeit inadvertently when he wasn't even looking for one. Both of our mentors provided us with good advice. Even better, they passed along our names to folks who hired medical writers, giving us opportunities to grow our businesses.

Now, you're probably wondering where you can find a talented writer who is willing to mentor you, especially if you aren't lucky enough to have a medical writer as a neighbor, like me. And that leads me to the next tip:

TIP #2:

Join the American Medical Writers Association.

I mentioned briefly in previous sections about AMWA and some of the benefits I received, but I want to tell you more. The best thing I did for my freelance career was to join AMWA, an international educational organization of professionals who work in the field of biomedical communications.

What does that mean? Well, biomedical communicators can be writers or editors or even presenters of health-science information. If you're looking for a mentor, AMWA is probably the best place to start.

AMWA has a formal educational component in the form of workshop courses, lectures, forums, and networking that allows writers to learn new skills and technologies. As an AMWA member, you can enroll in its core certificate program of courses that are given at the annual conference, at regional conferences, and at local chapter meetings. Once you satisfy the core program's requirements, you'll receive a Certificate of Completion. More important than the piece of paper, though, are the skills you'll learn from the experienced AMWA members who teach these courses.

And I'm not just talking about writing. AMWA courses address writing, editing, presentation skills, and business skills. They are also making a big commitment to provide science workshops, which seem to be popular among writers with and without science backgrounds.

My own mentor was and still is an AMWA member, and an involved one at that. She volunteers at both the local and national levels, acts as a guest columnist for the AMWA journal, and teaches noncredit courses. When I attended chapter meetings with Donna, I could see how valued she was by the membership. It was easy to see that she was a respected and talented writer, and I was lucky to have her around to mentor me.

I could go on and on here about the benefits of an AMWA membership, but I won't belabor the point. You can go to www.amwa.org to find out more. My coauthor has extolled the virtues of AMWA in his section of this book as well. For me, one of my favorite benefits of AMWA membership is the option to advertise in the AMWA Freelance Directory, where prospective clients can easily access my resume online. Check it out.

Even if Donna hadn't been my neighbor, I would have been able to find a good mentor through the relationships I built at AMWA. Still, it was important for me not to take advantage of Donna. When I was starting out, I wasn't able to attend every AMWA meeting or enroll in the core certificate program because of cost issues and the difficulties I had attending evening meetings when my children were young. That meant learning as much as I could about the business independently. Sure, Donna was, and your mentor will be (or should be), willing to answer my questions, but it really wasn't appropriate for me to call her every time I didn't know the answer. That becomes exhausting and, frankly, if I'm mentoring new writers who call me about every little thing without first trying to solve their own problems, I'll begin thinking twice about my decision to mentor them. I needed to find other ways to get answers. That brings me to my next tip:

TIP #3:

Buy the right desktop resources.

Thinking independently means having the resources you need right at your fingertips. One of the first things I did when I decided to become a medical writer was to go to the bookstore and buy reference books. As a new medical writer, I found these basic desktop references to be extremely helpful:

- A good medical dictionary (I use Dorland's, but others are available)

31

- A basic nursing procedure book (for me, Luckmann and Sorenson's *Medical-Surgical Nursing;* an old copy now out of print, but you can find others in your local bookstore)
- The most recent edition of the *American Medical Association's Manual of Style* (it's in its tenth edition now; ISBN 978-0-19-517633-9; make this one of the first books you purchase)
- A grammar and usage publication (try Edie Schwager's *Medical English Usage and Abusage*; ISBN 978-0897745901)

I also keep a copy of the *Physician's Desk Reference*, commonly known as the PDR, on my bookshelf. The PDR contains drug-prescribing information that is voluntarily supplied by the manufacturer. Whether I really need a hard copy of this reference in this day and age is debatable, since I can usually access the prescribing information for most marketed drugs online by simply going to my favorite search engine and typing in the drug's brand name plus the words prescribing information. If you prefer a book, as I do, by all means buy yourself a PDR and take the business deduction for it (keep your receipt). Just remember that a new edition of the PDR is published every year. It can become a costly venture to stay current.

Other publications come in handy, depending on what specifically I'm writing. I often find myself picking up *The Guide to Clinical Preventive Services* (ISBN 978-1883205131) or *Control of Communicable Diseases Manual* (ISBN 978-0875531892) for background information on certain disease states.

Of course, a wealth of information now exists on the Internet, if you know where to look. Most medical textbooks are available online through subscription databases. Some of these databases have hefty annual fees, but as an AMWA member I have online access to *Harrison's Online*, a basic medical text, as a benefit of membership.

When I was starting out, though, the Internet was in its infancy and was not readily available to the general public. No one was "surfing the net" for information, so all of my resources needed to be hard copy. Maybe that's why I still like to have a few of these reference sources on the shelf where I can see and touch them. Old habits can be hard to break.

Other electronic libraries exist, too, where you can access reliable and comprehensive information. Reviewing all of these databases and explaining how to use them efficiently is a book in itself, so I won't go in depth here. I will tell you that once the Internet became popular, my clients expected me to be familiar, at the very least, with PubMed, an electronic database provided by the US National Library of Medicine. PubMed includes more than 18 million citations of biomedical manuscripts from MEDLINE® (the electronic version of *Index Medicus*, the National Library of Medicine's monthly bibliography of the biomedical literature) and other life-science journals that date back to the 1950s. You'll find PubMed at http://www.ncbi.nlm.nih.gov/pubmed/.

Another database I find extremely useful is PDQ® (Physician Data Query), the National Cancer Institute's comprehensive cancer database. PDQ® offers cancer-information summaries about cancer treatment, screening, prevention, genetics, supportive care, and complementary and alternative medicine. Also available are a registry of cancer clinical trials from around the world and a directory of professionals who provide genetics services. The summaries are peer reviewed and updated every 6 months by editorial boards that review current scientific literature from more than 70 biomedical journals. This is one website you can trust, if you're looking for background information on cancer. You'll find it at http://www.cancer.gov/cancertopics/pdq.

Keep in mind, though, that there's a lot of "garbage" health care information available on the Internet that should not be acceptable to medical writers. We need hard science when we prepare documents, not personal opinions. So be careful when you're searching around for information and you come across blogs, unattributed websites, individual physician's websites, or so-called encyclopedic sites where anyone can write or revise entries. Good medical writers NEVER use this kind of information because it often lacks a credible science basis.

And speaking of online access, let's move on to my next tip:

TIP #4:

Become proficient with your computer software.

To be both effective and efficient, you need to know how to use your computer software well. This might sound like extremely basic advice, but you'd be surprised by the number of would-be writers who think the only things they need to know are how to type in words and create paragraphs.

I remember asking a writer to take a sequential list within a paragraph she had written and put it into bullet format. There was dead air at the other end of the phone. Finally, she admitted that she didn't know how to do it. Another time I instructed a writer to do a search and replace for a misused term. Again, silence followed by the question, "Can't the editor do it?" These were basic word-processing functions with which every writer should have been familiar. I was not asking these writers to do something difficult.

When I started out, I was a novice at using my computer. I knew only the bare essentials of word-processing software, and forget about using a mouse, but I forced myself to learn and learn quickly. At the time,

WordPerfect® was the preferred program and, as word-processing programs go, it was not very user friendly back in the early 1990s (at least in my opinion). Once Windows® became the preferred operating system, most of my clients eventually converted to the Microsoft Office® word-processing program. Transitioning from one program to another was challenging, but no matter how easy or complex these programs were, I had to learn them and learn them well if I wanted to work.

I'll be honest. Even now I don't know how to do everything with every one of the computer programs I use. But when I encounter a problem, I don't just sit at my computer wringing my hands. I don't call my client and say, "I can't." Instead, I call a colleague, usually my coauthor, Brian, who I consider a whiz at certain computer programs, especially Excel. He'll work me through my problem and I'm on my way. I do the same for him when he faces a software problem he can't solve. It works, and I would encourage all of you to cultivate this same type of relationship with one (or more) of your colleagues, or even your mentor.

Today, I find that my clients expect me to be proficient with these basic software programs:

- Microsoft® Office Word® word-processing software
- Microsoft® Office PowerPoint® presentation software
- Microsoft® Office Excel® spreadsheet software
- Adobe® Acrobat® (not just Adobe® Reader®, the free program, but the actual Acrobat® program that allows you to create and manipulate documents)

Why Adobe® Acrobat®, you might be wondering? Isn't a word-processing program good enough?

Let me explain a harsh reality in the world of pharmaceutical medical communications. The FDA has very strict regulations about pharmaceutical marketing that dictate what companies can and cannot say in their sales, marketing, and educational materials. When you are hired to write these kinds of products, for fact-checking purposes you will be required to reference the text extensively to indicate where you found the information. In other words, if you make a statement such as, "More than 10,000 Americans are diagnosed with writer's block each year," you will need to identify the citation (including page, column, and paragraph number) from which the data came. This is called annotating the text, and it takes a lot of time.

But not only will you be required to annotate the text of the document you are writing, you also will be expected to go back into the reference itself, which usually will be supplied to you in electronic form (most always as a pdf document), and highlight the particular information you cited in text. You'll be able to read the reference using Adobe® Reader®, but to highlight it, you'll need Adobe® Acrobat®.

When you have finished writing the manuscript, your written document plus the highlighted references then go to the pharmaceutical company's medical-legal review committee. This committee will go through your manuscript with a fine-tooth comb and compare your words with what actually appears in the highlighted references. This fact-checking process can be brutal, especially if you aren't careful about what you're writing, so paying attention to details is mandatory.

While I'm on the topic of computer software, let's review another tip:

Tip #5:

Update your software regularly.

Again, you may think I'm stating the obvious here, but I have encountered many writers over the years who work in outdated versions of software and this creates real problems, especially if you're working with a medical communications firm that expects you to create documents in very specific—and detailed—predesigned templates. Yes, I know that purchasing software packages is expensive. I recently spent several hundred dollars myself updating to Microsoft Office® Suite 2007 and I forked over another $300 on the latest Adobe® Acrobat® program.

You already know that new software updates often come with new computers when you purchase them, but sometimes those programs aren't the ones you need. Even if you don't have a reason to update your computer, at least update your software regularly. And always check with your clients to see what version they use. Just keep repeating, "It's a business expense…"

Staying up to date is also relevant to your internet service provider (ISP). With most projects, you will be sending and receiving large electronic documents, some with graphics that take up a lot of space. When I had my first ISP with a dial-up connection, it took hours to send files back and forth. That was perfectly fine then because most of my clients had the same type of connection.

I don't know if any readers still have a dial-up connection. If you do, you'll need to change your system because dial-up just won't do the job for you. Today my clients have dedicated servers and ISPs that can handle and transfer large files in seconds and they expect the same

37

capability from me. Although I don't have a need for my own server, I do have a fiberoptic service that transfers files in seconds.

Despite my updated fiberoptic service, sometimes I can't send or receive large files that contain a lot of graphics, even those supposedly within my ISP's capability. When this happens I use a free file-hosting service that permits me to upload files and then send a direct link to the recipient, who can download the file (it also works in reverse). One service I like is Mediafire (http://www.mediafire.com) because it doesn't require registration to use the site.

New software comes on the market frequently and my clients expect me to know how to use it. This means that I have to get up to speed rather quickly with these programs. And that leads me to my next tip:

TIP #6:

Always say yes.

When I began in this business, all I had written were those pieces in my portfolio, and my portfolio wasn't that varied. Plus, as I told you, I was not very familiar with computer software programs. How many clients do you think I would have attracted if I said no every time they asked me if I knew how to use a specific computer program, or if I had ever written a certain type of document? The answer is not very many.

So, when a client first asked me if I was familiar with Software Program XYZ, I said sure, even though I wasn't. Then I ran to the library in search of an instructional manual that showed me step by step how to use the software. I spent my own time learning how to become proficient in that program. Remember Lesson #3: *You have to spend money to make money.* Well, here I was, once again accruing unpaid time to learn a specific program that enabled me to attract additional clients.

I rarely said no, not because I wanted to lie, but because I had the confidence that I could figure it out. Plus I knew where to look for the answers. Before I wrote that first monograph, I contacted a colleague and asked her if I could look over some monographs that she had written. No matter what type of document I was hired to write, I always asked my clients for samples of the styles they preferred, and I used those as templates. Why reinvent the wheel? As I've become more experienced, I've found that with certain documents such as monographs and sales-training materials, my clients generally already have a style or format in mind when they hire me. And that's what I use.

When you read Brian's story, you'll see that he, too, asks for samples and then mirrors their styles and creative approaches. Honestly, it works. Pharmaceutical writing is not an exercise in creative writing. Companies—and their regulatory and medical-legal departments—have styles and formats they prefer. They usually don't want you to come up with something new and different because, most likely, it won't conform to FDA guidelines that dictate what can and cannot be said in medical communications. Brian does a great job of explaining these regulations in his section of the book.

Now that I've said that, let me add some clarity to this discussion about creative writing. In any type of writing, you have the content, and then you have the delivery or packaging. In medical communications it's not the content that's creative. The content is based on the science; however, the way the content is delivered or displayed is where the creativity comes into play. In this industry, you often have the opportunity to use your creative muscles to design a unique method of delivery for the dry scientific content.

In my opinion, it's easier to say yes to new, unfamiliar projects now than it was 15 years ago. Today you can find medical writing resources online, including books like this one and others that clearly describe the documents medical writers create.

If you want to be successful in this business you need to nurture your attitude so that you have the self-confidence to say yes when your phone rings and your clients ask you to try something new. Saying yes, as my coauthor emphasizes, gives you a chance to be a hero to your client. Being willing to attempt new projects gives you the opportunity to stretch yourself and add a new skill to your repertoire. You'll ultimately be more attractive to prospective clients if you've worked on a variety of projects, which brings me to another tip:

TIP #7:

Market yourself continually.

I often describe freelance writing as feast or famine. Some months I have to turn away work; other months I wish I had more. Rarely does there seem to be a happy medium. Regardless of how much work I have, I still market myself to prospective clients.

As I shared with you previously, I wasn't very marketing savvy when I started out. I depended completely on one company for work and, although that strategy worked for a while and it put me on the right path, it wasn't getting me to my ultimate destination.

Once I made the decision to attract other clients, my marketing tactics weren't elaborate. I simply made a list of potential clients and mailed them a cover letter along with my resume and business card, but I made a point of taking at least 5 hours each week to do marketing. Because I had previously worked in hospitals, I made sure those folks I had worked with before knew that I was now writing, since I wanted them to funnel as much work to me as possible. I also played up my clinical experience to develop a niche of writing patient-education materials.

Another benefit of my AMWA membership was the monthly Job Market Sheet distributed at the time by mail that identified freelance jobs that were available. Each month, if freelance jobs were listed, I mailed out my marketing packet to those prospective clients.

I still send out my resume and copies of selected clips to prospective clients even today, just to keep my name and experience in front of people who might need my services in the future. Of course, it's easier now since I can send everything electronically and don't have to lug manila envelopes to the post office as I did when I started out.

I need to insert a few thoughts here about confidentiality issues. The pharmaceutical companies for whom you will be creating materials get very cranky if you share their confidential materials and documents you produced for them with other agencies. For example, sales-training materials are highly confidential; never send these as samples to prospective clients. Be extremely careful about any samples you share that are not in the public domain and make sure you receive verbal and/or written permission to send out any documents you produced that were covered under confidentiality agreements you signed.

You may question this advice and wonder why this confidentiality issue is so important. If you're already a writer, you may be trying to equate confidentiality with copyright. You can't; they're separate issues.

Even though you write something for a pharmaceutical company, often by way of a third party such as a medical communications firm, you do

41

not own the copyright on that material and, usually, you won't be listed as the author. Whatever you wrote is considered to be work for hire, even if you haven't signed a piece of paper stating so. Some companies are much better than others at having you sign confidentiality agreements before you begin a project for them. But you need to be aware that, even if you haven't signed such an agreement, it is understood that the materials you produce become the property of the company who first contracted the work. You don't own the copyright.

If you're creating sales materials, much, if not all, of it will be for internal use only by sales representatives who will be selling the product or device you wrote about. Conversely, if you create materials for the purposes of continuing medical education that will be disseminated to clinicians in the field, these documents would be considered to be within the public domain. Keep this in mind not only when pulling together clips to show prospective clients, but when choosing documents to add to your website, if this is a marketing tactic you use. I personally think websites, if well done, are great marketing tools for medical writers. Just be careful when selecting the writing samples you post on your site to avoid any confidentiality issues.

The work-for-hire discussion logically leads to another concern about authorship and whether medical writers who contribute substantially to a manuscript should be listed as a coauthor. This so-called "ghostwriting" issue has been big news in the media recently. Read the accompanying sidebar for a more complete discussion.

SIDEBAR: MEDICAL WRITERS AND THE AUTHORSHIP ISSUE

If you read the lay media, you probably saw some of the articles that appeared in *The New York Times, Philadelphia Inquirer, The Chronicle of Higher Education, MedPage Today, and Reuters News* about so-called phantom authors and ghostwriters. This media attention was in response to articles and an editorial that appeared in *JAMA (the Journal of the American Medical Association)* that raised concerns about authorship and conflict of interest in manuscripts that were published in scientific journals. Unfortunately, the important contributions of medical writers got lost in the controversy. I'd like to add my perspective on this issue, making it clear that I have a conflict of interest, given that I'm a medical writer.

To better understand the concern and how it affects medical writers, let me provide you with some background. Pharmaceutical companies develop drugs and devices that they sell to make a profit. We all benefit from these developments. Consider the medications now available to treat diseases and the advantages this brings to society as a whole. Still, there exists a disdain for the pharmaceutical industry, even among some journal editors and writers, most likely—and this is just my opinion—due to the high costs associated with the drugs on the market today and the rising costs of health care in general. We all know that the pharmaceutical industry is not a nonprofit business, but seeing executives at most of the major pharmaceutical companies earn millions of dollars each year in salary and stock options makes folks question these high costs, particularly when the health care system in our country is in such disarray.

But I digress. To sell their products pharmaceutical companies obviously have to disseminate information about their products' efficacy and safety to prescribers. One way to do this is by publishing the results of industry-sponsored clinical trials in scientific journals. Keep in mind that drug companies **must** perform clinical trials on their products (thus the term industry-sponsored trial) as part of the FDA-approval process. Pharmaceutical companies are under strict regulatory requirements to publish clinical-trial data soon after the study is completed. Newer legislation requires results to be either published or posted on a public website within 2 years of the completion of the trial. Even more restrictive is the requirement that the sponsor of a clinical study submit a report for publication within 1 year of the last visit of the last patient who was enrolled in the trial. In other words, if the sponsor fails to publish the results within 2 years, the results technically can't be published at all.

Given these demanding timelines, pharmaceutical companies often don't have the resources they need to write the manuscripts, so they hire outside medical communications firms (also called publications-planning companies) to assist with the writing and submission of these manuscripts. These firms employ medical writers (freelance and on staff) to assist with manuscript development, but the writers' contributions may not always be acknowledged. This is where the unfortunate term "ghostwriting" comes into play. (I find this "g" word quite offensive; I won't use it again in this book.)

Because most individuals don't have a clear understanding of the role of medical writers, they assume that a medical writer writes the manuscript from scratch and an author tacks his or her name on it. This is not accurate. Medical writers collaborate with authors to develop a fair and balanced manuscript that communicates the key issues to the readers. Authors are the ones who identify the content to be included in a manuscript, who analyze the data, draw conclusions, abstract facts, and make comparisons with other scientific research that has already been published. Medical writers organize and explain content, condense data into tables and figures, and clarify confusing information. We are the experts at figuring out how best to present the content, whereas the authors are the experts at determining what the content should be. It's an important distinction that needs to be made. As a medical writer performing these tasks, I wouldn't expect to be named a coauthor, but I would like my contribution to the manuscript acknowledged.

Companies that assist in the preparation of scientific manuscripts, and the medical writers who work for them, are expected to follow good ethical practices and comply with criteria established by the International Committee of Medical Journal Editors (ICMJE) with regard to authorship and acknowledgement. (You'll find these criteria at http://www.icmje.org/index.html#top.) Although the trend at one point in time may have been to make the role of the medical writer invisible, today the importance of acknowledging everyone who makes substantial contributions to a manuscript is recognized. As a medical writer, I certainly want my role to be apparent and, like the authors, I'm happy to disclose any professional or financial relationships that would imply a conflict of interest. This is the cornerstone of the AMWA Code of Ethics.

I am proud to acknowledge that I'm a medical writer, and even prouder to say that I am a member of AMWA who strongly supports educating others about the important role of medical writers in the creation of scientific communications.

Entire books have been written about marketing, including online marketing, a particularly valuable tool for writers. If you have limited marketing experience, like I did, then you might find it beneficial to read a few of them. One title I've found extremely useful is *The Relationship Edge in Business* by Jerry Acuff with Wally Wood (ISBN 978-

0471477129) because it discusses how to build strong long-term relationships with your clients and colleagues.

I market myself in other ways, too, for example, by volunteering to be a guest speaker for local groups, including my local AMWA chapter. Most importantly, though, my reputation as an honest and forthright writer is the best marketing tool I have at my disposal. If you've worked in any kind of freelance arena, you know that marketing yourself continually can be exhausting, and attracting new clients takes a lot of time. Retaining the ones you already have is much easier, which is where my reputation comes into play. And that brings me to the final piece of advice I want to give you in this book:

TIP #8:

Honor your deadlines.

As a managing editor for a quarterly publication, I had a rigid deadline to follow in order to get the publication to our clients on time. If a freelance writer was even a few days late with a document, it caused a snowball effect that usually delayed delivery of the entire publication.

When I was hiring freelance writers, I wanted only those writers who turned in their work on time. Unfortunately, some freelances we contracted were not very concerned about meeting deadlines. I vividly remember one writer who called me the day her document was due to tell me she had been so busy she hadn't had a chance to even start it. Then she had the nerve to ask if I could give her 2 more weeks to finish it; this, after having given her the 3 previous weeks to do her job.

You've got to be kidding me, right? You better believe that she never wrote even one report for us. I never gave her the chance.

In all my years of freelancing, I missed one deadline, and that was due to poor time management on my part. I had taken on too many projects, and didn't have enough time to finish them all. When I called the client a few days before the deadline to tell her that I wouldn't finish the project on time, she was angry, and justifiably so. She grudgingly gave me an extension of a few days, which was all I needed, and I finished the project in time to meet that new deadline, but I never received another job from that client again.

Can you see where I'm going with this? No matter how skilled a writer you are, or how pleasant you are to work with, your ability to complete a project within a predetermined timeframe and within—or even under—budget is what your clients are going to remember about you. I had worked for this client for several years, always meeting my deadlines while doing commendable work. At one point in our relationship she even called me to tell me how pleased she was to have me freelancing for her company. She even sent me personal Christmas cards, complete with her home address. But despite all these good feelings I had generated, one misstep caused our relationship to end. No more projects, no more Christmas cards, nothing. She severed our connection cleanly, as though it had never existed. It was a loss I still feel at some level even today.

As my coauthor says, good news travels fast, but bad news travels faster. Don't ever underestimate the effect missing deadlines could have on your business and the relationships with your clients. Did my client talk to her colleagues at other firms about the great medical writer who freelanced for her or did she complain to them about the writer who couldn't get the job done on time? I doubt that she sang my praises over cocktails with her peers. Did that have an effect on my future freelance opportunities? Probably, but I'll never really know.

I almost missed another deadline, but I was smart enough by then to be a bit more proactive. When my older daughter developed a raging case of chicken pox, I immediately called the client for whom I was working at the time and told her of the situation. Even though the monograph I was writing wasn't due for another week, I wanted to be very up front with my client about the demands and time constraints I would be under. Although I wasn't planning to miss a deadline, the possibility existed that I wouldn't finish the project on time, especially if my daughter's disease progressed and my younger daughter developed chicken pox simultaneously. I knew that managing 2 itchy and feverish youngsters while writing a monograph would be too much to handle.

My client was extremely sympathetic. She gave me an extension that, as it turned out, I didn't even need. But she appreciated me being open and honest with her about what was going in my life. And I felt better knowing that I had some extra leeway, if I needed it.

I know that personal circumstances beyond your control will always interfere with your ability to perform your work. And situations will develop in your life that have the potential to cause you to miss a deadline. But if you keep your clients informed about these situations, usually you can avoid the bad feelings that might develop if you can't honor a deadline.

On the other hand, your client may bring certain issues to the table that will prevent you from meeting a deadline, no matter how diligent you are. My coauthor, Brian, does a great job describing project creep, that insidious beast that results in a deliverable that looks completely different from the one you originally agreed to write. If you're caught in the web of continual tweaks to a project's parameters, you need to be assertive and point this out to your client. Oftentimes, your client may not be aware of how these incremental changes are affecting your ability to complete the project on time and on budget. Never hesitate to say something like, "If you want a 4000-word manuscript instead of the original agreed-upon 2500 words, I'll need another 4 days to complete the job and another $2500." I firmly believe, and so does my coauthor, that clients need to understand how any changes in project parameters affect both deadline as well as budget. And the only person who can explain it to them is you!

Meeting deadlines is important to me because, in my opinion, it shows how seriously I take my business. It's a reflection of my professionalism and integrity. That's one of the reasons I get repeat business from my clients. And that accounts for a large proportion of my success.

Writing Mistakes to Avoid

That's my story about how being unqualified as a medical writer has led to a decades-long career that is still going strong. Before I conclude, I'd like to give you a few writing tips that will help your work look polished and professional.

If you recall, I previously told you about my mentor, Donna, editing my first medical writing assignment. She prevented me from making some of the common mistakes novice medical writers often make. I'd like to do the same for you.

In the years I've worked in this business, I've written and edited a lot of documents. Even when I know nothing about the writer, I can always tell if they're new to the business or if they've been around the medical writing block for a while. How? By the mistakes they make.

Here are some of the biggest mistakes to avoid when you start writing:

TEN WRITING MISTAKES TO AVOID

1. Writing in passive voice rather than active voice:
    a. Passive: Data were collected by the investigators.
    b. Active: The investigators collected data.
    c. Passive: Conclusions about the results will need to be made.
    d. Active: You will need to make conclusions about the results.

    Strive to use active rather than passive voice in your writing, since active voice is more natural and direct. Use passive voice

---

when the action, not who performs it, is important.

2. Writing "compared to" instead of "compared with." Don't ask me why, but for most medical writing purposes, it's always compared with.

3. Using "that" and "which" incorrectly. One of my biggest bugaboos; in my opinion this separates the novices from the experts. Here is a general guideline to follow. Use "that" with restrictive clauses that cannot be omitted from the sentence without affecting its meaning. Use "which" with unrestrictive clauses that can be omitted without changing the meaning of the sentence. When using "which" in this manner, always use a comma before it:
    a. INCORRECT: The results of this study provide data, which support the efficacy of the study drug for the treatment of psoriasis.
    b. CORRECT: The results of this study provide data that support the efficacy of the study drug for the treatment of psoriasis.
    c. INCORRECT: The medication that was administered to all patients resulted in an overall cure rate of 85%.
    d. CORRECT: The medication, which was administered to all patients, resulted in an overall cure rate of 85%.

4. Making the word "data" a singular noun:
    a. INCORRECT: The data shows that 55% of patients failed treatment.
    b. CORRECT: The data show that 55% of patients failed treatment.
    c. INCORRECT: This data appears in Appendix 2.
    d. CORRECT: These data appear in Appendix 2.

5. Using plural pronouns with singular antecedents like everyone and no one:
    a. INCORRECT: Everyone should complete their study diary.
    b. CORRECT: Everyone should complete his or her study diary.
    c. PREFERRED: Everyone should complete a study diary.

6. Using "regimen" and "regime" interchangeably. This is a big no-no, folks. A regime is a government that is in power. A regimen is a systematic or prescribed plan to follow. I know some online dictionaries suggest that you can use these words interchangeably; don't do it:
    a. INCORRECT: The drug regime included acetaminophen twice daily plus a protease inhibitor once a day.
    b. CORRECT: The drug regimen included acetaminophen twice daily plus a protease inhibitor once a day.

7. Using "affect" and "effect" incorrectly. It's important to remember that both of these words can be used as a noun or a verb; however, USUALLY, effect is the noun and affect is the verb. As a memory aid, I link the "e" in verb with the "e" in effect and remember that the verb (affect) does NOT have an "e":
    a. INCORRECT: The drug effects the limbic system.
    b. CORRECT: The drug affects the limbic system.
    c. INCORRECT: The affects of the drug last for 3 hours.
    d. CORRECT: The effects of the drug last for 3 hours.

8. Making the condition more important than the person:
    a. INCORRECT: One hundred asthmatics entered the study.
    b. CORRECT: One hundred patients with asthma entered the study.

c. INCORRECT: The diabetic patients measured their
    blood glucose levels before and after meals.
d. CORRECT: Patients with diabetes measured their blood
    glucose levels before and after meals.

9. Confusing the meaning of incidence and prevalence. If you want
    to be a medical writer, you need to learn the difference:
    a. Incidence is the number (or percentage) of NEW cases of
        something, usually a disease, per unit of population over
        a certain period of time.
    b. Prevalence is the number (or percentage) of existing
        cases per unit of population over a certain period of time.

10. Forgetting to use parallel construction:
    a. INCORRECT: The investigator's responsibilities include
        monitoring patients, to complete health forms, and meet
        with other investigators.
    b. CORRECT: The investigator's responsibilities include
        monitoring patients, completing health forms, and
        meeting with other investigators.

I could share many more writing mistakes I've encountered, and
committed myself, over the years, but that's the subject of another book.

Let me conclude simply by saying that I hope my story, as well as the
tips, mistakes, and lessons I've included have inspired you. Perhaps
you're teetering on the edge, dreaming about making a career change
or pursuing a long-held goal. Maybe you've been downsized or, with the
current economy in the shape it's in, you might need some extra cash
and you're considering freelance medical writing as a way to improve
your finances. This book is meant to give you some of the tools you

need to take the next step, to get you to move beyond dreaming and hoping, to taking action. Look for more titles in this series and read them all.

Section 2: Brian's Story

My Unqualifications

I've always been fascinated by the irony of not being able to get a job without experience, nor experience without first getting a job. I guess that's because, for most of my life, I've found myself in precisely that conundrum. Fortunately for me, I've never allowed an initial lack of experience to get in the way of my achieving my goals.

At the age of 9 I was perfectly qualified to be a 9-year-old. I had friends, parents, a younger sister, toys, TV, chores, a transistor radio, homework, and summer vacation. Little did I realize that this would be the last time in my life that I would actually be truly qualified to do what I was doing.

I don't recall exactly how my spiral into unqualification began. Perhaps it came upon me like one of those stomach bugs that 9-year-olds get. Or maybe it grew out of a bad case of the "I wants," although I do recall not getting those too often. My grandparents lived through the depression and taught my parents, as children, the value of a dollar, the hard work it takes to earn a dollar, and the importance of saving that dollar to pay for what you need and want. My parents' practical approach to finances rubbed off on me. As a result, I began looking to earn my first dollar at an early age

One day in early spring I went door to door asking whether I could cut people's lawns for money. After all, I had cut our lawn at home a couple of times and done a pretty good job, although my father may have disagreed with that assessment. Perfectionist! Imagine a 9-year-old today asking to cut your lawn. The liability issues alone make me shudder. But these were different times, and 3 of my neighbors actually took me seriously.

I wasn't much of a planner in those days. It wasn't until Saturday morning that I realized, for the first time in my life, I was unqualified to do what I was about to do. A peculiar feeling, but one that I have long since not only grown accustomed to, but have learned to embrace! I had no lawn mower, no edger or trimmer, no idea what to do with the clippings. I could have crawled back under the covers and waited for Monday. I could have asked my parents to bail me out of the mess. But I didn't. I created the situation, and I needed to see it through.

I got dressed, went to the first house that had agreed to take me on, and with the help of my customers I figured it out. Of course, that's a little easier to do when you're a cute little kid that adults are eager to take under their wing. They showed me how to use their mowers, where to add fuel, how to empty the bag, and what to do with the clippings. At the end of the day I had grass-stained sneakers, $15 in my pocket, and experience. I learned an important lesson that day:

LESSON #1:

It doesn't matter what you don't know. What matters is what you learn, and what people are willing to teach you.

As my coauthor, Cyndy, points out, another important lesson I learned, without realizing it at the time, was how to get paid while I learned!

At the age of 11 I became unqualified to deliver newspapers. I had never before been responsible for much of anything, let alone something I now know to be so near and dear to peoples' daily routines. Perhaps it's just the way I'm wired, but I took the responsibility very seriously. This was especially odd for someone whom no one would characterize as being either responsible or serious. I always made sure the paper was delivered on time. I even asked each customer where they wanted me to place their paper. Of course, each person wanted their paper placed in a different spot, but I soon discovered that this personal touch and extra effort translated into bigger tips. The observation that details matter and are integrally linked to value has stayed with me to this day, and I have found that it translates into just about every professional endeavor.

At 13, my burning desire to have a pet was all the unqualification I needed to get a job at a pet store. I'm glad to report that no animals were hurt during my tenure, although I know of a few tropical fish that experienced near-death, out-of-tank experiences. Through this job, I learned valuable lessons about dealing with people, like how to listen to what customers want. I also learned about life-and-death deadlines. If I didn't get the inventory fed on time, the consequences truly could be tragic. While I've never heard of someone dying as a result of a missed medical writing deadline, I have seen missed deadlines kill future job opportunities (gladly not my own).

By 17, I had also wangled my unqualified behind into positions as a stock boy at a local department store, a line cook in the cafeteria at a roller bearing factory, and a clerk at a supermarket. Although I didn't realize it at the time, in addition to teaching me the ropes about the specific job I was doing, each of these positions was subliminally teaching me one very important thing: what I didn't want to do for the rest of my life.

I have great respect for people who make their living doing things that I prefer not to do, and I'm sure there are many people who prefer not to do what I do. That's what makes working so much better than food gathering. In early civilizations, people ate what they gathered, nothing more. While today we're supposed to be more advanced, in my estimation, working is still food gathering, except now we gather one thing, then barter for everything else we need or want. I am committed to leveraging my food-gathering skills, so that some day I won't have to gather to barter to eat and enjoy my life. But that is the subject of another book in our series.

After spending so many years doing jobs it turned out I really preferred not to do forever, and with only an impending high school diploma paving my future, I realized I needed a better plan.

Then came college.

The path my college career took can best be described as similar to the path that Billy in the *Family Circus* comic strip takes to find something that was right next to him all along. Under the chair, behind the curtains, pet the cat (yes, I'm easily distracted), out the back door, swing on the swing (very easily distracted), talk to the neighbor, back in the front door, grab a cookie (hmmm, ADHD?), look in the drawer, watch TV, and, oh yeah, there's what I want to do with my life!

My college career can be summarized as follows:

Theatre major.

Science major.

Psychology major.

Communications major.

What had been sitting right next to me all along—heck, it was always staring me in the face—was my love for writing. I had an equal passion for poetry and term papers, although one won me a bit more favor with the ladies than the other. (I won't tell you which one it was, but I will tell you that I dated some pretty practical women.) This passion, of course, unqualified me to be a professional writer. So I decided to focus my career as an advertising writer.

In the fall of my junior year of college, I, like all the juniors of the late 1970s, new-age, Ramapo College of New Jersey, a pioneer of multidisciplinary education, had to apply for our majors in order to prepare for graduation and be accepted for our chosen degrees. This involved going before a special board and explaining how the courses we had taken and the courses we were planning to take were going to get us where we wanted to go. Now I had a problem. I had taken so many different types of courses before I decided what I wanted to do, who in their right mind would accept this as an educational track?

I'm telling you this story because it was my first career epiphany. This was the moment when all of my unqualified years, dating back to that first blade of grass I cut for money, congealed into a force too powerful to be denied. I explained to the board that I was going to be an advertising writer, and that since the clients for whom I would write may be in any of hundreds of different industries, the more I knew about everything, the better prepared I would be for my career.

They bought it. And that's when I learned my second important lesson:

LESSON #2:

It is easier to get forgiveness than it is to get permission.

Had I asked my career counselors in advance to allow me to take all these different courses—assuming I had the clarity of knowing that I wanted to be a writer all along—they would have laughed me out of the school. Instead, they forgave me my *Family Circus* path because I had a solid rationale for it (albeit developed post hoc).

Little did they realize that they unleashed a monster, for now I knew I could do anything.

I did go into advertising writing, first for a small ad agency in Manhattan. Gene, the owner, had far more vision than I for what I was capable of doing. I will talk more later about the importance of mentors, as does my coauthor Cyndy. Anyway, in addition to trusting me to be the agency's only staff writer, Gene also allowed this unqualified neophyte to teach himself (on the job, for pay) to be a media director and an account manager! The agency's clients were predominantly in the entertainment industry, which was perfect for me given my passion for acting, singing, and dancing. We were promoting concerts at Carnegie Hall and Lincoln Center, off-Broadway shows, and ballet companies. We also launched a major arts-oriented cable TV network.

Afterward, I spent a few years as a writer in the retail industry. This experience taught me more about being an effective writer than anything I've ever done. The blinding pace of the retail-advertising environment allows time for either thinking or doing. Not both. It taught me how to quickly envision the end result so I could focus on getting there and ignore everything irrelevant to that goal. Hint: this is a major-league skill for those who wish to be successful freelance medical writers. Another familiar phrase comes to mind that is aptly appropriate for my retail-writing experience: what doesn't kill you makes you stronger. Trust me, I got out by the skin of my teeth.

I had just taken a job with a new company that specialized in marketing retail electronics when my first daughter was born. She was just 3 days old when I was called into the General Manager's office. I thought he

62

was going to congratulate me, perhaps give me a raise or promotion. Instead, he informed me that at the end of the week, everyone in the company was going to be laid off. The division was being closed, and the GM wanted to keep about 10 people including me to help close things down. He offered me a position to stay with the company, but I would have to relocate my family to Chicago or California. My wife, Andrea, and I thought long and hard about it. After all, my decision wouldn't just affect me, and now it wouldn't affect just me and my wife. We had a child to consider, too.

I came to the realization that I would be better off unemployed where I was than to relocate and risk being laid off later in unfamiliar surroundings without a support network. This was a pivotal moment in my life, although I wouldn't fully appreciate the importance of the decision I had made until many years later, when I read Robert Kiyosaki's excellent book *Rich Dad. Poor Dad* (ISBN 978-0446677455). What I had done with my decision was choose the security of myself over the insecurity of a staff position.

The decision was made, but I knew I needed to do some planning. So a few weeks before I left the company, I started calling friends who were also writers in the retail industry to let them know I was about to become available for freelance work. It was fall, and I knew retail-advertising departments would be exploding with work for the holidays. If I was going to keep money coming in, I had to go where I knew the money would be, even though I really wanted to get out of the retail industry.

I filed for unemployment for the first and only time in my life on my 28th birthday. Not a great present, I assure you. But I ended up having so much freelance work that I never collected. I freelanced every day through the holidays and into the new year, when I started looking for a new writing opportunity. Something that wasn't retail. Something that would be more intellectually stimulating and creatively challenging. Something that I could do and still have time for a life.

That's when I found an opportunity to write for an ad agency that specialized in animal-health pharmaceuticals. And that is what made me unqualified to be a medical writer.

To say the least, my path to this profession has been circuitous. My point in giving you this background is not to say that I am unqualified to do what I do for a living, although that is probably quite apparent. (Shhh! Don't tell my clients!) It is to say that you can be successful in the end regardless of how you got started.

Most of us come to our chosen professions via our own unique route. As my coauthor, Cyndy, explains, she came to freelance medical writing from science with little background as a writer. I have come to freelance medical writing as a writer with little background in science. There is no right way or wrong way, only *your way*. It is our hope that this book will give you the confidence you need to make your way the right way for you. Other books in our series will then give you the tools you need to see your way through to a successful career in medical writing—whether you choose to freelance, or to go to the "dark side," my literary nod to working as an employee. Read on!

The Awkward Years

The day I interviewed for the writer position with the animal-health ad agency, I had no idea how I would convince them of my ability to do the job. My portfolio could not have been less scientific, less medical, or less animal. I pondered this all during my drive to their office, hoping that something brilliant would come to me. Nothing did. When I was called in for the interview, I smiled and exchanged pleasantries. I kept looking for something in my background that I could leverage. The person I was meeting with held my resume in front of her. It was like a giant 2-page billboard screaming "UNQUALIFIED." I figured that if I could keep her eyes off the page she wouldn't notice.

Then it dawned on me. The common thread between me and the position for which I was interviewing was advertising. That's what they did, and that's what I did, too. As for the subject matter, I decided I would dust off the logic I had used to justify my college degree to see whether it would "play in Poughkeepsie." I told the person I was interviewing with that in my short career I had written about many different things, and that in the process, I had taught myself how to be a quick study. But this was a different application of the same logic, so I should have anticipated a different response. I didn't.

"Prove it," she said

Thinking quickly, I asked her to give me one of the current assignments on her desk, and a little time to get back to her. Whether I reeked of confidence or stupidity I can't say, but I knew there was no middle ground. If I wanted the job, I had to do something. Once again, I had created a situation by telling someone I could do something despite being apparently unqualified. Now, once again, it was up to me to see it through. I sealed the deal (and my fate) by adding that if she didn't like what she saw, she wouldn't have to pay me, but that if she did like it, she would have to pay me and (hopefully) seriously consider hiring me.

One side note here: neither my coauthor, Cyndy, nor I advocate working for free. Ever. What I proposed to my potential employer may seem incongruous with that philosophy, but consider this: although I said the work would be free if it wasn't acceptable, I had no intention of working for free because I intended to do a great job. In the freelance environment, you need to be that confident of yourself and your abilities, particularly if you are just breaking in. As they say, put up or shut up. Of course, just as it is important to know what you can do, it is equally (if not more) important to know what you can't do. I will address that important lesson in a moment.

My challenge was to create an ad for the use of a branded diuretic in dogs. At the time, of course, I had absolutely no idea what a diuretic is. In case you don't know either, a diuretic is a type of medication used to treat certain cardiovascular diseases such as hypertension (high blood pressure) and congestive heart failure. Diuretics work by removing excess fluid from the body, which is why they are often referred to as "water pills."

The audience for the ad would be veterinarians. I was given scientific background on the product, a creative brief describing what the overreaching message for the ad should be, and a few examples of previous ads that had been done for the product. These examples were invaluable. I mirrored their language style and creative approach, and did my best to understand and then incorporate the information I had been given to deliver the message the client wanted. By the end of the project, I even had a slight understanding of diuretics and their therapeutic application. My head was swirling with all the new information I had packed so quickly into my brain.

66

I delivered the project and waited eagerly for feedback. She had me wait in another room while she and her colleague reviewed my work. When they came to get me, their faces were completely blank. I couldn't get a read on what they were thinking, and that made me all the more nervous. I think they could tell that I was nervous, too. They began with the customary "Well, we've reviewed your work and bla bla bla..." that usually accompanies rejection. But then they both grinned and said that while I had made some obvious mistakes because I didn't know what could, and could not, be done in pharmaceutical advertising (read more about this in the sidebar), I also brought some unique thinking to the project they found refreshing.

SIDEBAR: WHAT YOU CAN AND CAN'T DO IN PHARMACEUTICAL ADVERTISING

Although many people seem to believe otherwise, pharmaceutical advertising is one of the most heavily regulated industries of which I'm familiar.

To give you an idea of what I mean, imagine what it would be like if automobile manufacturers were held to the same regulatory requirements. It would take an average of 8.5 years to develop a new car, at an average cost of $802 million dollars including the cost to conduct studies to investigate whether or not the new car is as safe and reliable as competitors' cars.

The manufacturer would have just 5 years of patent exclusivity after the new car is approved for market to earn back all their development costs plus overhead (to say nothing of profit) if the car is a totally new design; just 3 years if the design is similar to other cars but supported by new studies—before competitors could start legally copying the car and selling it for less (which they could afford to do because they didn't have all the development costs).

Then, any time the manufacturer mentions the car name in communications, they have to tell potential customers about all the bad things that could happen to them by using the car—like running out of gas, getting a flat tire, sliding on ice and rear-ending a semi, slamming into a snow bank, hitting a moose, breaking down on the interstate at rush hour, driving off a cliff on a tight mountain curve, and getting hit by a drunk driver.

If the manufacturer tells people in their advertising that they can drive the new car on mountain roads, and the car isn't expressly approved for use on mountain roads, or if the types of mountain roads depicted in the ads appear more treacherous than the roads for which the car was approved, the ads could be yanked and the manufacturer could be fined millions of dollars. And if people buy the car using government-subsidized money, such as Social Security or federal unemployment, the fines for misrepresenting the car could be millions of dollars higher.

In the showroom, sales people can't say anything about the new car that customers can't read for themselves on the window sticker.

Although it may sound like I am, please don't think that I'm bashing the US Food and Drug Administration (FDA). The FDA is the main regulatory body of the pharmaceutical industry. In fact, it is the regulations that guide pharmaceutical development and communications in the United States that make the US pharmaceutical industry one of the safest and most admired in the world. Make no mistake, there are equivalent regulations guiding communications in the medical-device industry, too.

My point is that there is a regulation for everything the pharmaceutical industry does—from developing its product, to training its sales force, to promoting its product. Pharmaceutical manufacturers are continually scrutinized, and they can be severely punished for doing anything wrong.

As a freelance medical writer, you need to know about these regulations and how they affect what you write. You don't have to know every word and letter of every law by heart, but you need to know what you can and can't say because of them. Some people find the regulations dampening to their creative spirit. I personally gain great satisfaction from knowing that because of these regulations, I am able to write medical communications materials that are responsible, informative, educational, and beneficial to everyone involved.

The regulations are far too extensive (and boring) to include in this book, but here are some links you should check out to learn more:

- **fda.gov** (the US Food and Drug Administration)

- **oig.hhs.gov** (the Office of Inspector General, OIG Compliance Program Guidance for Pharmaceutical Manufacturers)

- **fda.gov/cder/ddmac** (the Division of Drug Marketing, Advertising, and Communications)

- **accme.org** (the Accreditation Council for Continuing Medical Education)

The animal-health ad agency paid me for the freelance project *and* offered me the job, which I started the following Monday. Once on staff, my first assignment was to learn how to fix the ad I had written, and to see the ad all the way through client approval. I learned something new

69

every day for the next 4 years, and I was paid for doing it. The company paid me to learn about therapeutic areas and treatments, the language of medical communications (for example, the difference between *effectiveness* and *efficacy*), the rigors of pharmaceutical company approval processes, and the dos and don'ts of the legal and regulatory environments that govern medical communications. Of course, a lot of what I learned during those years was specific to animal health and not applicable to human medicine, but learning that I had the capacity to learn all this information without my head exploding was the best education of all. This experience taught me an important new lesson:

LESSON #3:

With good input and direction, <u>plus</u> a good example or two, you can do almost anything.

My start as a medical writer was in animal-health pharmaceuticals, but I soon began branching out by freelancing on the side in other medical areas. That's one of the great things about medical communications; if you're good, your name gets around. Of course, the bad thing in medical communications is that if you're not good, your name gets around, too.

The ad agency I was working for rented a spare office to Rebel, a unique guy with a brilliant white handlebar moustache that seemed to fit perfectly with both his face and his name. Rebel had a small ad agency of his own specializing in medical diagnostics. He utilized our company's art department for design and production, and although I didn't know it, he was watching me progress in my skills as a medical writer. Once he had enough confidence in me, he asked me to assist him on a freelance basis. At the time he was willing to pay $50 an hour, which seemed like an incredible amount of money to me at the time. I gladly took on the extra work because I wanted the extra money, and I also wanted to break into other areas of medical communications. Rebel was willing to pay me to learn.

I started writing promotional materials and manuscripts in the field of medical diagnostics. When the manuscripts were published, they even named me as the author! While that wasn't enough to get me into a fancy Hollywood party or an exclusive Manhattan nightclub, it sure felt pretty special to me.

No mention of manuscripts would be complete without a discussion of the role of medical writers in the development of manuscripts that ultimately appear in medical journals (erroneously, and offensively, often referred to as "ghostwriting"). The issue concerns the writing of medical journal articles by a medical writer who is typically not acknowledged for his or her contribution, nor held to the same standard as the attributed authors for identifying conflicts of interest. At the heart of the issue is the legitimacy of the content. Personally, I believe it is unfair to assume that medical writers are inherently biased and willing to compromise themselves ethically and morally. I also believe the problem (and ultimate resolution) rests with those who contract and benefit from our services, who gain by not acknowledging the role of medical writers.

My coauthor, Cyndy, has an excellent discussion of this still-controversial issue in her section of this book. The American Medical Writers Association (AMWA) has published a *Position Statement on the Contribution of Medical Writers to Scientific Publications* to which I wholeheartedly subscribe. This statement can be found on the AMWA website at http://www.amwa.org. In addition, I recommend you read the position statement from the International Society for Medical Publication Professionals (ISMPP) on the role of the professional medical writer, which was published in *Current Medical Research and Opinions,* Volume 23, Number 8, 2007:1837-1840.

Rebel paid me to learn (and write) about blood cell counters, blood culture systems, and thyroid function tests. It was amazing. Everything I was writing about was something I had not only never written about before, but something I had not even *known* before!

To show you how important it is to develop relationships if you want to be a successful freelance medical writer, and to prove that great opportunities are everywhere, in the span of just a few years Rebel went from being just a guy who rented space from my boss, to my first freelance medical writing client. In fact, after a few years, Rebel closed his business, went to work for someone else, and brought me into that company, which became a huge freelance client for me for many years.

It just occurred to me that if you are not in the medical or scientific fields, you may not know what a manuscript is. That's why Cyndy and I have created this series of books. The goal of this first book is to show you that you *can* become a successful freelance medical writer regardless of your background and qualifications. The other books in our series will show you *how* to become a successful freelance medical writer by giving you the knowledge you will need to run your business efficiently and effectively and to write the different types of materials that medical writers write.

One day, a project came into the ad agency I was working for on the treatment of canine sepsis. Sepsis is a serious bacterial infection that spreads throughout the body in the blood. It is very serious and can often be fatal. The client had a new class of drug that required a high-science sell. The reference materials I received from the client made my brain ache, and each time I thought I had made sense of something, I realized I was only more confused. Writing the project was one of the most terrible experiences of my life. I felt like I was floating helplessly in a sea of confusion with no rescue ship in sight. Finally, I told my boss that I was concerned about being able to do a good job, but we were close to deadline and there was no way out. I had to complete the project. I did complete the project, but I didn't complete it well. Needless to say, the client wasn't pleased, and we had to bring in a writer with more experience and knowledge in the therapeutic area. I had made a big mistake:

MISTAKE #1:

Not knowing what I couldn't do.

As I mentioned in Lesson #3, a good writer can do almost anything with the right input and direction. The key word there is *almost*. I was in over my head on the canine sepsis project from the beginning, which is not a mistake. But it took me too long to realize I was in over my head, which was a mistake. This brings me to my first tip:

TIP #1:

Know what you know, and know what you don't know.

Admittedly there is a fine line here. On one hand, you've got to step out of your comfort zone if you want to be successful in advancing yourself. But on the other hand, if you go too far and can't deliver, you will hurt

73

more than just the project on which you're working. You can also damage your reputation, to say nothing of losing the potential for additional work from that client. And don't discount the people that client knows. Good news travels fast, but bad news travels even faster.

The animal-health ad agency was a great opportunity for me to discover my inner science geek, and enabled me to develop the confidence that I could learn and write about almost anything. I was in a great spot. A comfortable spot. I guess that's why it had to come to an end.

I've never really been comfortable being comfortable. I like change. And I like taking on a challenge, overcoming it, and getting on to the next challenge. My coauthor, Cyndy, was reading an early draft of this manuscript and asked me to clarify this section a bit. She said she was confused about why my position with the ad agency had to come to an end when everything was going so well. She proposed that I explain the rationale for my leaving. Perhaps that "even though I was working hard and earning enough money for my wife to be a stay-at-home mom, we weren't getting ahead." I would love to be able to write those words, because they were true. In fact, because I always worked for small companies, I never had a retirement plan, so we were actually falling behind with each passing year. But that isn't the reason why I left.

My dad passed away about a year earlier. It was a devastating blow, and I admit I had a difficult time dealing with it. What hit me the hardest was that my father had worked very hard his entire life, postponed a lot of joy. At 55 years old, just when he was finally free of kids and all the expenses and concessions that kids require, just when he and my mom could have begun reaping the benefits of all they had worked so hard to have, my dad was gone and my mom was alone. I knew that I didn't want that to happen to me and my wife. The more I thought about it, the more I realized that although I would probably keep inching ahead with the company I was working for, inching ahead was neither fast enough nor far enough. I wanted to do better with my life, exponentially better, and the only way I could do that would be to work for myself.

My first daughter was almost 4 years old and my second daughter was just 11 months old. We had $2500 in a savings account. My wife, Andrea, had not worked outside our home for 4 years. I had to give up my company car, which meant having to get a new car. And our mortgage was due in 20 days. That's when I quit my job.

Into The Light

Monday morning, August 19, 1989. That's the day I started working for me. I started a business, a small ad agency just like the ones I had worked for during so much of my career. I incorporated my company as Bass Advertising & Marketing, Inc., a name I have retained to this day although my business is now quite different.

My last day on the "dark side," which is what I prefer to call the evil that is staff employment, had been the previous Friday. Today, instead of heading out to the car and straight into traffic, I poured a cup of coffee and headed straight into my basement. Sitting down at my desk, I faced my computer and my telephone, and the fact that I had 3 people upstairs who were counting on me to know what I was doing. I had a plan. But if you define "knowing what I was doing" as "having a full appreciation for the gravity of the situation I had precariously put myself and my family into, plus having all the skills and knowledge I would need to make this adventure a success," I was clueless. To paraphrase Gene Krantz, lead flight director for Mission Control during the legendary Apollo 13 flight, "Failure was not an option."

Over the next several years, I learned many valuable lessons:

LESSON #4:

Never underestimate the motivating power of fear.

Fear made me focused. The thought of not being able to pay the bills forced me to think clearly and act decisively; to get work today and get that work done right away, so I could put money in my pocket within 30 days or less. I was the sole wage earner in my home, so I had no one else to rely on to help pay the bills. That was the challenge I created for myself, and the challenge I had to address. How did I put money in my pocket so quickly? The answer is not from the business I was trying to build, my ad agency. I made money quickly by freelancing evenings and weekends as a medical writer. I was working nearly nonstop, marketing and developing ad agency business by day, and getting that new business done, and freelance writing at night and on weekends.

My wife would have gone back to work if we needed her to, and we discussed that on many occasions. She did eventually go back to work because she wanted to after our children were older. After spending many frustrating years herself on the "dark side," she is now doing something for herself (and ourselves), too. She is building a restaurant business, which is something she has wanted to do for a long time; however, during the early years of my business, our goal was to see whether we could maintain our quality of life, which included my wife being a stay-at-home mom.

My coauthor, Cyndy, was motivated by fear, too, although hers was a different situation than mine since her income was secondary to her husband's. This is a good example of the gender gap that Cyndy discusses in her section of this book, although I believe the scenario would play out similarly for a husband whose income is secondary to his wife's. This is occurring more often now that men are feeling more confident in the role of stay-at-home dad and more women are leading the corporate charge. Cyndy's fear may have been different from mine, but it was no less urgent, important, or real. In the sidebar, I take this discussion of gender gap one step further, into the field of medical writing.

SIDEBAR: THE GENDER GAP IN MEDICAL WRITING

My coauthor, Cyndy, writes about there being a gender gap. I believe this is unfortunately still true throughout much of the working world. But it should not be true in medical writing, and it *certainly should not* be true for freelance medical writers. Perhaps I feel so strongly about this because I have 2 daughters, and my wife and I have tried to raise them with the confidence to never allow themselves to be limited by the archaic and idiotic beliefs of others. There are enough challenges for all of us to overcome on the road to success, including those we put in our own way; however, I feel just as strongly about inequality in the workplace (or anyplace!) because of race, religion, sexual orientation, perceived disability, or any other prejudice. Sorry, this is just one of those subjects that makes me pull out my proverbial soap box.

The AMWA Salary Survey has consistently shown that the gap in income between male and female medical writers is dwindling. It is still there, but the gap has narrowed over the years that the survey has been conducted. Personally, it surprises me that there is a gender gap at all in medical writing. I think there are actually more female medical writers than male medical writers. Can't the women just overpower the men? I'm joking, but watch out guys. The days of the gender gap are (hopefully) numbered.

What really amazes me, though, is that there is a gender gap among freelances. In a staff scenario, if a company pays a woman less than a man to do the same job, and the woman has comparable credentials, that's discrimination. But in a freelance scenario, if a woman charges a client less for her services than a man, and they are equally qualified to get the job done properly, I can't believe it's because of her gender. That would be self-discrimination! I suspect it's because she's just not

http://www.theaccidentalmedicalwriter.com

aware of her value—and that can happen to anyone, male or female.

I have given many presentations on pricing and freelance fee negotiation. People ask me why I am willing to openly discuss this typically "taboo" topic. "Aren't you afraid of giving away your secrets to a competitor?" they often ask. I see things differently. To me, the biggest competitor is a great writer who doesn't value her- or himself properly. I want every freelance medical writer to earn as much money as they can. This way, we benefit individually and collectively.

Fear made me flexible. I couldn't afford to hold out for the "plum jobs," I had to take every opportunity that came my way, and make it work to my advantage. Of course, this also led to one of the biggest mistakes of my career, one that I have made over and over again, and will probably still make again:

MISTAKE #2:

Not trusting my instincts.

Good, bad, and sometimes ugly, my instincts have gotten me where I am today—to the point of being a successful freelance medical writer. So it makes no sense to me that sometimes I pay absolutely no attention whatsoever to those instincts. Especially when the stench of death is all over a potential assignment.

I once got a call from a company that wanted me to take on a quick project for them. They flattered me with things they said they had heard about me. When I asked them about the project, they weren't clear about anything but the deadline. BIG RED FLAG! And, of course, they didn't have much of a budget either. My instinct screamed "RUN!" but my bank account said "Sure."

The project remained poorly defined. I trudged onward. Of course, because I wasn't clear about my direction, it was difficult to avoid writing in circles. For that reason, the project also took much longer than it should have taken to complete. My client, a medical communications company that is no longer in business, by the way, didn't even read the first draft. They just forwarded it to their client, who pounced on it like a lion. My first draft was "hideously off target," my client's client claimed. Needless to say, I was toast. Although the lack of direction wasn't my fault, my client sacrificed me (and my reputation) to their client to save themselves. The next day, I began incorporating into my estimates a statement informing my clients that my deliverable is to their specifications, which puts the onus on them to make sure the specifications they provide are on target.

Of course, if a client is intent on hanging you out to dry, there's little you can do to stop them. That's why it's important to trust your instincts, to spot bad projects before they go bad and avoid them like the plague. You might miss a few good projects along the way. But in my estimation, it is better to lose a few opportunities to make money than it is to risk losing your reputation.

That said, it can still be difficult to turn away a project you think could be deadly. Several years ago I came across a saying that is both true, and a wonderful tool for determining whether you should avoid a project. It has enabled me to avoid many mistakes. Here's the saying:

There are 3 ways to work:
    Good.
    Cheap.
    Fast.

Clients can choose any 2.
    Good and cheap won't be fast.
    Cheap and fast won't be good.
    Fast and good won't be cheap.

If a client wants all 3, RUN! Personally, I run when clients want the cheap and fast option too, since my reputation for delivering high-quality work is always on the line.

Fear energized me. I have always worked for small companies, so I know what it's like to wear many hats and to always be busy. But I have never worked so hard as when I started working for myself. That's because:

No work = No income

This seems like a pretty simple equation, yet I know plenty of brilliant people who work on the "dark side" and just don't get it. They're the reason many good companies fail. When you get a paycheck every week regardless of what you accomplish, you are betting that the collective productivity of other people's work will be enough to cover your salary, too. But if enough people have an unproductive day, or week, or month, or year, all that's left is the "float" between accounts payable and accounts receivable to cover your paycheck.

"Float" is the period of time between when money comes into a company in the form of revenue (accounts receivable), and when it flows out of the company in the form of expenses (accounts payable). In healthy companies, "float" doesn't matter because there is more money coming into the company than there is flowing out of the company to pay bills and salaries. But in companies that are not healthy, there isn't enough money coming in to cover expenses. That can happen for a lot of reasons. Maybe sales are down because there is less demand for widgets this month. Or maybe there is a downturn in the economy, so people are holding back on buying new widgets. Maybe there is a new competitor who is selling a better widget, or selling their widget at a better price. But perhaps the reason there isn't enough money coming in is because productivity is down while fixed expenses, such as salaries, taxes, utilities, rent, and debt service, remain steady.

Productivity is a silent killer of companies, especially smaller companies. You often can't see it, and you certainly can't taste it or smell it. When the money gets tight, salaries go to the front of the line to be paid, and bills go to the back of the line to be paid whenever there is enough money left over to pay them (or a vendor makes enough noise about their overdue invoice). If the situation doesn't improve, eventually there isn't even enough money to pay salaries. In short, the "float" eventually sinks. That's when the downsizing usually begins.

Fear made me strong. Every day, I wake up out of work. Not really. In fact, I'm usually juggling 4 or more projects at a time. What I mean is that every day it's up to me to make my business successful. If I fail, I have no one to blame but myself. When I succeed, I have no one to reward but myself. I like those odds. I have always known that I could go back to the "dark side" if things didn't work out. That was my safety net. But over the years I have strengthened my confidence in myself to the point where no one could pay me enough to work for them on staff. I find the uncertainty of being able to lose my job even when I've done everything right, because something happened that was out of my control, and to find myself unemployed, demoralized, and out of practice to be very risky. There is no risk in working for myself because I know I can do it, and do it well.

82

When I went on my own in 1989, I started a small, full-service advertising agency. I worked in the past for ad agencies that were specialized, and that collectively gave me a wide range of experiences. I decided to build my ad agency to be very diversified, and thereby reduce my company's risk of being at the mercy of any one industry should that industry fall on troubled times.

My ad agency's first client was a fertilizer manufacturer that catered to both lawn care professionals and homeowner customers. My ad agency's second client was a new, single-branch financial institution that had just opened up in the area. I happened to have a lot of financial writing experience from an ad agency I interned with while I was in college. As the company grew, my ad agency client list expanded to include clients in the electrical, transportation, parking, and pharmaceutical industries. I call these my "agency clients" because my company did a lot more than just provide writing services for them. I had a whole team of people working with me to serve these clients. I even had a small staff. In addition to doing my own writing, I was hiring graphic designers, photographers, typesetters (before the age of computers), and printers. We were even "buying media," which is slang for placing ads that we had created for clients in magazines, newspapers, and the electronic media, which did not yet include the Internet (Al Gore, Vice President of the United States, had not yet invented it).

But more about that growth in a few minutes.

You may remember that in the beginning, I, and my family, needed money fast. I had just quit my job for what seemed like no good reason (consider the argument against parachuting—why would anyone jump out of a perfectly good plane?). So to make ends meet, just like I had done many times in the past, I decided to freelance as a writer to make extra (and fast) money. In the early days, it was freelance medical

83

writing that helped me pay the bills. I picked up work right away from my friend, Rebel, and he soon opened the door for me with another company for additional freelance writing work. Then the floodgates seemed to open.

One day, a freelance photographer named Jerry, whom I frequently hired for my ad agency business (and always made it a point to pay on time even when I couldn't afford to buy paperclips), called. Why did I include that little parenthetical? Because it explains why Jerry did what he did for me. The valuable lesson that I learned from this experience has stayed with me, and has become even more important to my success today:

LESSON #5:

If you want good people to work for you, pay them well and pay them on time.

This lesson certainly holds true for how I want my freelance medical writing clients to treat me, and how you should want your freelance clients to treat you. It also holds true for how I treat the people who work for me today. It makes sense, but you would be surprised how many clients don't pay on time. How many clients don't understand, or don't appreciate, that people who work for themselves, who own their jobs, really can't feed their families or pay their mortgages if they don't get paid on time.

By treating my photographer friend, Jerry, professionally, which means paying him the high fee he deserved, and paying him on time after every project, Jerry didn't hesitate to do something nice for me. Here's what he did.

When Jerry called, he told me that the creative director at a good client of his, an ad agency that specialized in orthopaedics, was coming in for a shoot. Jerry wanted me to stop by and "deliver an envelope" so he could introduce me. Of course the chance meeting was contrived because there was no "envelope" to deliver, but I am forever indebted to Jerry for opening the door for me to this new opportunity. I handed Jerry a 9x12 envelope with a piece of paper inside on which I wrote the words "Thank you!" He introduced me to Richard, who without his realizing or anticipating it, became my one and only true mentor.

Richard was (and still is) a wonderful medical writer. When we met at Jerry's studio, he told me that Jerry mentioned to him I was doing some medical writing. He asked me whether I would be willing to stop by sometime to show him my portfolio. He might have some freelance work for me. A week later I met with him. It was a good meeting, although I think I spent far too much time apologizing for my lack of medical writing samples. Then he pulled a brochure out of a pocket at the back of my portfolio that I had forgotten was even there.

The brochure was a promotional piece I had written years before for the entertainment ad agency I worked for in New York. The brochure was for a touring theatrical production called GROUCHO! based, as you might guess, on the life of the great Groucho Marx. I was embarrassed that Richard found the piece in my portfolio, more so when he insisted on reading every page.

I explained that when I started writing the brochure I had already written many just like it and was frustrated that such brochures were generally all written the same boring way. To make the brochure more entertaining and hopefully more effective (and also more fun to write), I

85

took a different approach. I researched Groucho Marx, watched every Marx Brothers movie I could get my hands on, and read several books Groucho himself had authored. Then, instead of writing yet another boring brochure promoting a show, I wrote the brochure as if Groucho himself had written it—complete with first-person quips, asides, and commentary.

The brochure had helped the show sell out quickly for its entire run. Richard confided in me several years after we had been working together that if the *GROUCHO!* brochure had been the only sample in my portfolio that day, he would have hired me for freelance work just the same. For him, that piece demonstrated that I wasn't afraid to commit myself to a project, that I had the ability to learn along the way, and that I had the courage to apply that knowledge in a fresh new way. That's when I learned my next lesson:

LESSON #6:

Relevance is relative.

When I am counseling people who are new to medical writing, I am often asked, "How can I make my experience relevant?" The irony is I am usually asked this question by people who have far more relevant experience in the medical field than I. I usually respond by encouraging them to see themselves differently. To look at the skills their experiences convey that are relevant to the task at hand, even if the experiences themselves are irrelevant. This is what my first and only mentor, Richard, saw in me. Cyndy writes about the importance of a good mentor. I wholeheartedly agree! Some mentors provide guidance, some provide opportunity. In my opinion, the best mentors provide both!

AMWA (the American Medical Writers Association) has also been a great mentor to me. Every person I have met, every workshop I have attended—even the many workshops, roundtables, and sessions I have given at AMWA meetings and conferences— have contributed immensely to my knowledge and abilities as a medical writer. I have also had the privilege of serving both my local AMWA chapter and the national organization in many capacities over the years. The more I have gotten involved, the more I have gained by being an AMWA member. I can't recommend more emphatically that if you want to be a professional medical writer—whether freelance or on the "dark side"—you must become an active AMWA member. The organization's certificate program is outstanding, and overshadowed (if that's possible) only by the value of the many networking opportunities that AMWA membership provides. I know my coauthor, Cyndy, feels the same way about AMWA. If you want to learn more about AMWA, their website is a great place to start: www.amwa.org.

Owning A Job

I want to start this section by explaining the difference between owning a job and owning a business, a difference that I wouldn't learn for myself for nearly another 10 years, and after initially heading in the wrong direction. I learned the difference from Robert Kiyosaki, author of the best-selling series *Rich Dad, Poor Dad.* I highly recommend his books and those of his colleagues. To explain the difference between owning a job and owning a business, let me start at the beginning.

Most people don't *own* jobs, they *have* jobs. They work hard all their lives, spend most of what they earn, save what little they can, and hope to retire someday to live off Social Security, a pension, and the money they gain by selling what most people believe is their biggest asset, their house (if it's not already overleveraged in debt). For all their working lives, and all their retired lives, they will be at the mercy of people, corporations, programs, and dynamics that are either completely or mostly beyond of their control.

Owning a job is better than *having* a job because you're in control of your primary source of income. You can't be fired on the whim of a boss or board of directors. You are responsible for all the successes as well as for all the failures. You have to solve all the problems, do all the marketing, buy all the office supplies, make all the coffee, and do all the work. You also have to do all your own investing for your retirement. The important thing to understand is that even though you're the owner, it's still just a job. If you don't work, you don't get paid. It's that simple. By owning my freelance medical writing job, I had all the rights, privileges, and responsibilities of ownership, but I could never stop working because I was the only person making money for me.

Having never worked for big corporations, I never had profit sharing, stock options, or a 401(k). Over the years I've put money into a SEP IRA, and my wife and I have committed ourselves to building assets that will work for us when we decide to stop working. That's what owning a business is all about—having assets (including other people) that work for you, and why owning a business is different from (and better than) owning a job. A business works *for you.*

When you own a business, other people are working to earn your company (and you) money. When you own a business, you still have all the rights, privileges, and responsibilities of ownership, but now you don't have to make all the money yourself. Another benefit is that a business is an easier asset to sell than a job. Of course, while I now have a great team of freelance medical writers who work with me on an as-needed basis, I still spend 30 or more hours a week writing myself.

In a future book in our series, Cyndy and I will address how you can use a freelance medical writing business to break free from having a job. We'll show you how you can leverage your freelance job to build a freelance business. And we'll help you harness the power of your freelance medical writing business to achieve your personal financial goals.

So how did I go from owning a business, my small ad agency, to owning a job? It was the summer of 1993, and I had a decision to make. Since starting my ad agency in 1989, the business was growing very nicely. I had about a dozen clients in a range of different industries and a small staff. At the same time, since starting freelance medical writing in 1989, demand was increasing steadily for my services. Since I couldn't add any more hours to the day, I either had to stop freelancing so I could build my ad agency to the next level, or I had to stop running my ad agency so I could make more time for freelance medical writing. After a lot of soul searching, I decided that the world didn't need another small ad agency, but that my abilities as a medical writer were both unique and valuable. This is the decision that took me from owning a business to owning a job. It's also a decision that I have never been sorry for making. I didn't know it at the time, but by focusing on what most interested me, and what I did well, even though it wasn't what I expected to do with my career, I was laying the foundation for a business that I could truly be passionate about, and that I would ultimately be successful at building. In the next section, I'll explain how I built my freelance writing job into a business.

Once I was able to focus full time on my freelance medical writing business, clients who were pleased with my work were happy to refer me. I also initiated an aggressive marketing program. There are many great ways to market your freelance medical writing services. None of them is right or wrong, just different. The way I chose to market myself was based on my personality and goals, and what I felt most comfortable doing. You should never choose a way to market yourself that doesn't come naturally, because the likelihood of failure is much higher. For example, if telemarketing makes you uncomfortable, cold calling potential customers (that is, calling someone on the phone who doesn't know you and isn't already seeking your services) is probably not a good idea. My approach to marketing myself was to develop a direct-mail campaign that I could produce myself. I sent the direct mailing to a select group of targeted potential customers whom I identified through my own research, a group that was a small enough that I could manage to follow up with a personal telephone call. Then I fired off a new mailing every 3 months. (Direct-mail marketing will be discussed in a future book in our series.)

Thanks to my targeted promotional campaign, I was able to get back into pharmaceutical writing, but this time on the human-medicine side, as well as continue to build my writing experience in orthopaedics, diagnostics, and devices. I found that my clients were better than me at articulating the benefits I brought to the table for them, so I listened. Indirectly, they told me which niches I filled for them, what problems I solved, and why they preferred to work with me rather than other freelance medical writers. Then I incorporated what they were saying about me into what I was saying about myself in my promotional materials. By listening, I also realized that as freelance medical writers, we're not really writers. We're problem solvers. We just happen to solve our clients' problems with medical writing. Let me explain.

Every company's desire is to utilize their staff writers first. After all, they are already paying their salaries and benefits. Freelances aren't usually called in until staff resources are either tapped out or determined to be insufficient for the project at hand. In either case, the realization usually comes late in the game, and the company has nowhere to turn. That brings me to my next lesson:

LESSON #7:

Every time the phone rings, it's a chance to be a hero.

I love it when my phone rings because it means someone has a problem they need me to solve. When I solve it, they appreciate me, pay me, and call me again the next time they have a problem. They refer me to their friends and colleagues who also have problems to solve, and they take me with them when they move to a new company because they know they can trust me to help them solve the problems that await them there. I make my clients look good. That's my job. And I do it with medical writing.

By the late 1990s I was on top of the world. I had all the freelance medical writing work I could handle, great clients, and a solid stream of revenue. I reached "critical mass." That is, I had enough clients and work that there was always a new project coming in. I didn't have to market myself anymore to get work. So did I stop marketing myself so I would have more time to write? Of course not! That would be crazy. Where do you think Coca Cola would be today if they stopped marketing? Or GE? These are some of the largest and most successful corporations in the world, and they know that to stay on top they must keep themselves on their customers' minds. To put this into a freelance medical writing perspective, I offer this lesson:

LESSON #8:

The time to look for work is NOT when you need it.

I know some freelances who work on one job at a time and turn down all other opportunities that come along. They don't even start looking for the next job until the one they're working on is finished. I think that's crazy and a lot more work. Think of it this way: it takes a car a lot more time and energy to go from 0 to 60 miles per hour than it does to go from 30 to 60 miles per hour. Freelance medical writing works the same way. If you disappear from your other clients' radars every time you're working on a project for someone else, they can forget about you. At the very least, if they have a project while you're unavailable, they have to find another writer to help them, and perhaps they'll like that new writer more. Working this way, you can find yourself out of work for weeks at a time. Depending upon how many projects you are able to do in a year, you could actually spend more time out of work than working. It can be tough to pay the mortgage that way.

I prefer never to let my velocity dip. I do that by juggling several projects at a time, and by constantly looking for new work even though I don't need it. This way, I stay on the top of all my clients' minds.

In fact, at the time, my clients only wished I could clone myself so I could handle even more of their work. You might think that I owe this all to being a great writer. While I hope that's partially true, I know it's not the whole story. In reality, I owe my success to several other factors in addition to my writing ability. There are plenty of great writers out there, many of whom I'm sure are much better than me. The difference between us, which makes me more successful, is that they make mistakes that I don't make. Consider this analogy:

> Four runners start a race. One runner is faster than the others, one is stronger than the others, one knows the route better than the others, and one is competent in all categories but not the best in any. As the race begins, the runner who is the fastest pulls immediately out in front, but makes a wrong turn and soon becomes lost. The runner who is the strongest takes the lead, but soon becomes distracted and stops running. The runner who is most familiar with the route is now in the lead, but trips and falls over an unexpected bump in the road. The runner who is competent but not the best crosses the finish line and wins the race.

If your first thought after reading this story is "Gee, I don't have to be good to succeed as a freelance medical writer," you completely missed the point. In fact, the opposite is true, you need to be the very best that you can be in both what you do and how you do it, if you want to succeed as a freelance medical writer. The point I was trying to make with this story is that, often, the best way to succeed simply is not to fail.

93

I can't tell you how many times I see or hear about freelance medical writers who shot themselves in the proverbial foot. That is, they made an avoidable mistake that cost them the job, or maybe even the client. If you can avoid making the mistakes that others make, and you are good in all areas of what you do and how you do it, you can succeed as a freelance medical writer.

This brings me to my next lesson:

LESSON #9:

If you want to win the race, you've got to cross the finish line.

I see many freelance medical writers make avoidable mistakes. Their mistakes usually have nothing to do with the writing itself, but with the business end of how it is delivered. These mistakes can hinder the outcome of the project, and often cost the writer in lost future projects with that client, as well as referrals. Along the way, they lose sight of the goal for which they're writing. Or they get distracted by other projects or personal interests and forget to keep moving toward the deadline. Or they trip over details they either didn't see coming or thought were unimportant. Below is a list of some of the classic mistakes I see freelance medical writers make. I would like to thank them for their mistakes because they have helped me to get to where I am today.

TEN CLASSIC MISTAKES
FREELANCE MEDICAL WRITERS MAKE
(FOR WHICH I THANK THEM EVERY DAY)

1. Calling the day (or the day before) a project is due to say:
   a. I need more time
   b. I need more input
   c. I need more direction
   d. I need more money

2. Missing the deadline

3. Producing an inferior product by being:
   a. Unqualified to write on the subject or at the level required
   b. Unfamiliar with the medium (print, video, audio, interactive, Web)
   c. Unaware of the relevant legal or regulatory requirements
   d. Unaccustomed to writing for the target audience

4. Missing the client's target message

5. Not asking for, or worse yet, not demanding, all the information that is needed to do the job

6. Not returning the client's phone calls…immediately

7. Not following up after delivery of the first draft

8. Not telling the client when you are going to be out of town or otherwise unavailable

9. Sending an invoice that is for more than the agreed-upon fee

10. Not learning from your mistakes

One of the secrets to my success is that I work very hard to not make the mistakes that other writers make. The following tips will help you avoid making those mistakes, too:

TIP #2:

Promise what you will deliver, and deliver what you promise.

When I prepare an estimate, I describe exactly what I expect to receive from my client in the form of input and direction, and I describe exactly what I am going to do with that input and direction in terms of the deliverable I will provide. When my client approves my estimate, it automatically becomes my contract, protecting us both. Providing this level of detail ensures that I have understood the project correctly, and that both I and my client understand our respective responsibilities. It also protects me against project creep, which I like to describe as an insidious process by which small, incremental "tweaks" in project parameters result in the delivered product looking nothing like the proposed product even though no major changes were made. Big changes are easy to track, and everyone expects pricing to be adjusted accordingly, for example, when a monograph is expanded from 16 pages to 32 pages, or when a detail aid is expanded from 4 pages to 12 pages. (Monographs and detail aids are topics for future books in our series.) Project creep is much more difficult to pin down, but this is what it sounds like:

> ***"I know I said this would be a 3,000-word manuscript, but we can go up to 4,500 words"*** (That's up to 50% more work for free!)

"Do whatever it takes." (Passes the responsibility onto you for poor project definition!)

"The client just sent over another truckload of references. See what you can use." (Nobody's managing the client!)

"We just got feedback from 3 more reviewers who were on vacation while the manuscript was being routed." (A hidden round of revisions!)

Project creep can make it difficult for you to be paid appropriately for the altered deliverable if you aren't protected—especially if it's not the deliverable, but what it took to get there, that changed. The way to protect yourself is with a detailed estimate. The more specific your estimate, the better able you are to call out even minor changes in project parameters, enabling you to adjust your estimate accordingly.

TIP #3:

Deliver on time, on target, and on budget; first time and every time.

I spent many years in staff positions being responsible for hiring freelance talent. Writers, designers, photographers, I found almost all of them to be the same. With few exceptions, freelances don't care as much about the client, the project, the timing, the budget, or the process as the person and the company who is hiring them. I have found that being totally committed to delivering on time, on target, and on budget makes my client's life easier. And that's my goal, to make my client's life easier. Because the more confident my client can be in handing over a project to me, the more projects they'll hand over.

I'm Fired, And Rehired

So there I was, at the top of the world in the late 1990s, or so I thought. Until I realized I wasn't at the top of the world at all. I was on top of a mountain, a mountain I was proud to have climbed all by myself. But when I started looking around, I realized there were taller mountains to climb.

By 2001, I had built my freelance medical writing business to the best and the biggest it could be with me doing all the work, but I couldn't make it any bigger. My clients were constantly asking me to clone myself, so I knew there was more work to be had. I just couldn't see how to make it work. Every solution I thought of seemed too impractical. Infeasible. Then one day, while enjoying a relaxing day with friends at the beach, it dawned on me. I was getting in the way of my growth. *I was the problem.* So at the end of 2001, I fired myself.

I contacted a few of my best clients, people whom I had seen (and helped) build their businesses from staffs of just a few people to staffs of dozens and more. They now had departments and infrastructures, Human Resources (HR) and Information Technology (IT), company picnics, and promotion tracks. I respected their ability to create successful companies. I explained to them that I was looking to get out of my way for awhile, to see what I wasn't seeing, and to learn from them. For an honest day's pay I would give them an honest day's work. Then I fired myself. I carefully closed down my freelance medical writing business, and went to the "dark side." It lasted 11 months.

It might have lasted longer, but the education I received came much sooner than expected. It also came in a completely different way than I had expected. I expected to gain insights about managing clients and staff, strategies about pricing and promotion, and techniques for planning and implementation. What I learned was that I already had a pretty good handle on those things, and the clients I respected were not doing anything different from what I might have done. So why were they able to successfully build their businesses beyond themselves and I wasn't? The lesson I learned was simple. Elegant. And I never saw it coming:

LESSON #10:

Never stop taking risks.

Ever since I risked everything by quitting my staff job with the animal-health ad agency back in 1989, I thought I was taking a risk every day by being on my own. I was wrong. As a matter of fact, quitting that job was probably the last big risk I had taken. I had forgotten that back then there were a million sound reasons why what I was doing wouldn't work, but I refused to pay attention to them. I *made* it work.

The unexpected education I received from my 11-month return to the "dark side" in 2002 was that I wasn't able to build my freelance medical writing into a business because I was playing it safe. I was doing what I already knew I could do, freelance medical writing, thinking every day it was as daring as the first day I started doing it back in 1989. In fact, that was the last time it was daring. I had raised the bar on myself and then I was consistently coming in under it. I was so fixed on what was working that I had become afraid to try something new. To take a chance. I could only see why my ideas might not work, instead of having the guts to see whether I could *make* them work.

I had known for a long time that the only way to build my freelance medical writing business into an actual business was to have other writers working for me. I had always resisted the idea because I thought, "If I'm already earning at the top of my field, how can I bring in other writers who are also at the top of their field to work with me, and make any money?"

As I have stated before, to get good people you have to pay good money, so asking good writers to reduce their rates to work with me was out of the question. In fact, I hope that any of the incredibly talented writers who work with me on my team will tell you that I go out of my way to make sure they earn everything they can.

Armed with the knowledge of what I had to do, and (finally) the courage to do it, I parted ways with the company with whom I had now worked on staff for 11 months in an honest and amicable way. It was late 2002, and I was ready to start taking chances again. The chance I took was to start hiring other great freelance medical writers to work with me on a freelance basis, which is what I had long thought would be financially impossible. My goal is to always keep myself busy writing first. But when a project comes in for which I am either too busy to take on, or for which another writer on my team is more qualified, I subcontract the work to that writer. The relationship between me and the writers on my team is clear with my clients, meaning that my clients always know when another writer is working with me on a project. In fact, very often they ask for one of the writers on my team by name.

I finally had the guts to attempt what my brain had been telling me for so long was impossible. I learned that clients *value* great work and are *willing* to pay for it because it makes their lives *easier*. Today, the writers on my team with whom I have the privilege of working are well trained, highly educated, experienced, and talented (in short, they are much more "qualified" than I am). They understand, as I do, how to keep

101

clients happy and coming back for more. As it turns out, my fears that hiring other writers to work with me wouldn't work were unfounded. I have gone from owning a freelance medical writing job to owning a freelance medical writing business with other people working for me— which is a pivotal step in achieving my own personal and financial goals.

Unqualified And Successful. You Can Be, Too

Today my freelance medical writing business employs a core team of writers who are all expert, accomplished, professional, and successful in their own right. I love being able to bring in great people to work with me and then turn them loose to do what they do best. My clients love that, too. They know they can count on me and my team to solve their problems with accurate, rigorous, high-quality medical writing, and to consistently deliver for them on time, on target, and on budget. My coauthor, Cyndy, was the first writer to join my team. That's how we met. We were introduced by Cyndy's friend, neighbor, and mentor, Donna. Of course, Cyndy has many other clients of her own. There's security in that diversity. We are constantly bouncing ideas off each other, asking each other for advice, and working together on projects.

In this book, Cyndy and I explain how we both became successful freelance medical writers despite starting out unqualified to do what we now do for a living. Our stories are different. Our approaches are different. Our goals are different. The lessons we've learned along the way are different. Cyndy knew science and learned to write. I knew writing and learned the science. But the end result for each of us is the same. We are each achieving the success we desire. We each have the freedom to enjoy our families and balance our professional and personal lives. And we each have the security of being the only ones responsible for our success.

The reason we've told you our stories is to let you know that, regardless of your background and experience, you can be successful as a freelance medical writer, too. Is medical writing for everyone? Definitely not. Is freelancing for everyone? Certainly not. Can our experiences, stories, lessons, and tips help you if you want to work for yourself, even if it's not in the medical writing field? Absolutely. Because many of the things Cyndy and I have learned and shared with you in this book are fundamental to the success of building any freelance business.

This book is meant to give you the confidence you need to get started and the foundation to be successful—no matter how you personally define success. Perhaps you're a health care professional who loves to write or a writer who is interested in health care. Perhaps you're a stay-at-home mom or dad looking to return to the workforce, or you're looking to retire without coming to a screeching intellectual halt. Maybe you're looking for a career change or for a way to achieve a better balance between work and play. And maybe, just maybe, you're looking to take your first step toward financial independence by breaking free from the "dark side" of working for someone else. Freelance medical writing can help you make your dream a reality. The other books in our series pick up where this book leaves off. We hope you will read them all, and that you, too, will realize that once you were unqualified to be a successful freelance medical writer.

Good luck!

Section 3:
Medical Writing
Resources

About This Section

W e've provided a lot of information in this book. And we know sometimes it can be confusing. To make things easier for you, we've compiled this resource section. Here you'll find a listing of the resources discussed in this book, as well as other resources we believe you'll find useful. Whether you're new to medical writing, or you already have some medical writing experience under your belt, becoming familiar with the resources that follow will make you even more valuable to your clients.

We've divided this section into 3 categories: books, databases and websites, and organizations. We also provide you with a description of the phases of drug development, and information about *The Accidental Medical Writer* series.

Be assured that between the two of us, the books listed here are on our bookshelves and the electronic sources we describe are plugged into the "favorites" sections of our browsers. We use these resources on a daily basis. We wouldn't tell you about something we ourselves don't use or need.

These are the resources we wish we had known about when we launched our freelance medical writing careers. It took us years to discover and learn about them all, and we are sharing them with you to save you that precious time. But make no mistake, we're discovering valuable new resources constantly!

Take some time now to examine these books, explore these websites, and search these databases. You'll be amazed at the wealth of information you find.

Books

- *American Cancer Society Textbook of Clinical Oncology, 2nd Edition*, edited by Walter Lawrence and colleagues; ISBN 978-0944235102. This useful resource provides information on the various types of cancer, including incidence and prevalence, diagnosis, treatment, and outcomes.

- *American Medical Association's Manual of Style, 10th Edition*; ISBN 978-0195176339. This guide for authors and editors is indispensable on your bookshelf. With few exceptions, most clients you'll be working for will follow this style guide.

- *The Anatomy Coloring Book* by Wynn Kapit and Lawrence M. Elson; ISBN 978-0071466332. Whether you use your colored pencils or not, this handy interactive resource makes learning anatomy as easy as coloring by numbers.

- *Control of Communicable Diseases Manual* by David Heymann; ISBN 978-0875531892. From actinomycosis to yersiniosis, if you're looking for a description of a contagious disease and how it's controlled, you'll find it here.

- *Dorland's Illustrated Medical Dictionary*; now in the 31st edition; ISBN 978-1416023647. Another indispensable resource in our libraries, this dictionary provides definitions for almost any medical term you'll come across.

- *Goodman and Gillman's The Pharmacological Basis of Therapeutics* by Laurence Brunton, John Lazo, and Keith Parker; ISBN 978-0071422802. This essential reference book explains the physiologic principles behind the rational use of drugs in clinical practice.

- *The Guide to Clinical Preventive Services, Second and Third Editions* by the US Preventative Services Task Force; ISBN 978-1883205131. This book is considered to be the premier reference source on the effectiveness of clinical preventive services, such as screening tests for the early detection of disease, immunizations, and risk-reduction counseling. Find more information at: http://guidetoclinicalpreventiveservices.com.

- *Harrison's Principles of Internal Medicine*; ISBN 978-0071466332. From pathobiology, signs, and symptoms to disease management, this reference resource contains the latest medical information upon which physicians base their medical decisions.

- *Health Literacy from A to Z. Practical Ways to Communicate Your Health Message* by Helen Osborne; ISBN 978-0763745509. An indispensible resource for medical writers who are interested in writing for lay audiences, written by a recognized expert in the field of health literacy. This book provides practical strategies and tangible solutions for writing clearly and concisely on a wide range of medical topics for diverse audiences.

- *Medical English Usage and Abusage* by Edie Schwager; ISBN 978-0897745901. In this reference text, the author, who is a long-time member of AMWA, an AMWA fellow, and the author of the *Dear Edie* column in the *American Medical Writers Association Journal,* reviews some principles of medical communications and provides explanations to enhance understanding.

- *The Merck Manual of Diagnosis and Therapy, 18th Edition* by Mark Beers; ISBN 978-0911910186. This resource, the world's largest-selling medical text, is just one of a series of Merck Manuals created by the pharmaceutical giant, Merck & Co., Inc. Merck provides the content of these health care books, written for medical professionals as well as consumers, on the web for free at www.merckmanuals.com. No registration is required, and use is unlimited. Online publications are updated continuously to ensure up-to-date information.

- *The New Oxford English Dictionary*; ISBN 978-0195170771. Every writer needs at least one updated dictionary to which they can refer.

- *Orthopaedic Dictionary* by Stanley Hoppenfeld and Michael S. Zeide; ISBN 978-0397513116. This specialized dictionary defines terms you are not likely to find in typical medical dictionaries and contains hundreds of helpful illustrations.

- *Physician's Desk Reference* by Thomson PDR; published annually; http://www.pdr.net. The PDR, as it's commonly known, provides drug-prescribing information for every FDA-approved agent.

- *The Relationship Edge in Business* by Jerry Acuff with Wally Wood; ISBN 978-0471477129. Jerry, a former pharmaceutical sales representative, provides tools and advice to enable you to build strong relationships with your clients and business associates.

- *Rich Dad. Poor Dad* by Robert Kiyosaki; ISBN 978-0446677455. Actually a series of books, the *Rich Dad. Poor Dad* series are motivational resources everyone thinking about starting their own businesses should read.

Databases and Websites

- **AccessMedicine.** McGraw-Hill's subscription-based online medical library with resources that are updated daily: http://www.accessmedicine.com

- **ClinicalTrials.gov.** A free, searchable registry of federally and privately supported clinical trials conducted in the United States and around the world, maintained by the US National Institutes of Health: http://www.clinicaltrials.gov

- **The Cochrane Database of Systematic Reviews.** This database is a collection of evidence-based reviews that summarize the results of clinical trials on a variety of health care interventions. Summaries of the reviews are free; however, full-text reviews are available only to subscribers: http://www.cochrane.org/reviews

- **Drugs@FDA.** A free, searchable and browsable database from the US Food and Drug Administration (FDA) that provides details about brand name and generic prescription and over-the-counter human drugs for most drug products approved since 1939. This catalogue includes patient information, labels, approval letters, reviews, and other information. You can search for drugs by drug name, active ingredient, or FDA application number: http://www.accessdata.fda.gov/scripts/cder/drugsatfda/

- **The Electronic Statistics Textbook.** Produced by StatSoft, Inc., this extremely complete website reviews elementary statistical concepts and provides an in-depth review of specific areas of statistics, including definitions of various statistical terms: http://www.statsoft.com/textbook/stathome.html

- **Health Services/Technology Assessment Text (HSTAT).** HSTAT, a free, searchable, online database, is part of the expanded Health Services Research Information Program coordinated by the National Library of Medicine's National Information Center on Health Services Research and Health Care Technology (NICHSR). HSTAT includes a variety of full-text documents that provide health information for health care professionals, policy makers, payers, and consumers: http://www.ncbi.nlm.nih.gov/books/bv.fcgi?rid=hstat

- **Lab Tests Online.** A peer-reviewed, noncommercial website that provides easy-to-understand explanations of the various laboratory tests administered today. You can search the site by test name, condition or disease, or patient type: http://www.labtestsonline.org

- **MAUDE.** Manufacturer and User Facility Device Experience Database, also known as MAUDE, is a database you can search for information about medical devices that have malfunctioned or caused a death or serious injury. It includes voluntary reports since June 1993, user facility reports since 1991, distributor reports since 1993, and manufacturer reports since August 1996: http://www.fda.gov/cdrh/maude.html

- **MD Consult.** A fee-based database that brings the leading medical sources together into one integrated online resource; free with membership to AMWA; however, certain conditions apply: http://www.mdconsult.com

- **Mediafire.** A free file-hosting service that enables transfer of extremely large data files; does not require registration before using: http://www.mediafire.com

- **National Center for Health Statistics.** A compilation of statistical information about diseases, health care services, and other vital statistics in the United States. If you want to find out how many people were treated for heart attacks in hospital emergency rooms during a certain frame, for example, you'll find that data here: http://www.cdc.gov/nchs

- **National Guidelines Clearinghouse.** A free, public resource for evidence-based clinical-practice guidelines, an initiative of the Agency for Healthcare Research and Quality (AHRQ). This site identifies all clinical-practice guidelines that have been developed and provides direct links to most of them: http://www.guidelines.gov

- **National Quality Measures Clearinghouse.** A free, public repository for evidence-based quality measures and measure sets, sponsored by AHRQ: http://www.qualitymeasures.ahrq.gov

- **The Orange Book.** A listing of generic equivalents for prescription medications. The Electronic Orange Book is updated daily as new generic agents are approved: http://www.fda.gov/cder/ob

- **PDQ® (Physician Data Query).** The National Cancer Institute's cancer database offers information on diagnosis and treatment of the different types of cancer: http://www.cancer.gov/cancertopics/pdq

- **PubMed.** A searchable database of more than 18 million citations from MEDLINE® and other life science journals for biomedical articles back to the 1950s: http://www.ncbi.nlm.nih.gov/pubmed/

- **PubMed Central.** A free digital archive of biomedical and life sciences journal literature: http://www.pubmedcentral.nih.gov/about/intro.html

- **US Census Bureau.** A database of all the census information the government collects: http://www.census.gov

- **US Department of Health and Human Services.** A compilation of a variety of downloadable publications and information about drugs, diseases, and public policy, with helpful links to other sites: http://www.hhs.gov

Organizations

- **Accreditation Council for Continuing Medical Education (ACCME).** The ACCME is the body that accredits institutions and organizations that offer continuing medical education (CME) for physicians and other health care professionals. The ACCME seeks to identify, develop, and promote standards for quality CME: http://www.accme.org

- **Agency for Healthcare Research and Quality (AHRQ).** The AHRQ is the health services research arm of the US Department of Health and Human Services (HHS). It examines how people get access to health care, how much care costs, and what happens to patients as a result of this care: http://www.ahrq.gov

- **American Medical Writers Association (AMWA).** The professional organization for biomedical communicators: http://www.amwa.org

- **Division of Drug Marketing, Advertising, and Communications (DDMAC).** DDMAC reviewers are responsible for reviewing prescription drug advertising and promotional labeling to ensure that the information contained in these promotional materials is not false or misleading: http://www.fda.gov/cder/ddmac/

- **International Committee of Medical Journal Editors (ICMJE).** This group of general medical journal editors meets annually to update guidelines for writing journal manuscripts; these guidelines are known as the *Uniform Requirements for Manuscripts Submitted to Biomedical Journals: Writing and Editing for Biomedical Publication*: http://www.icmje.org

115

- **International Society for Medical Publication Professionals (ISMPP).** This is a not-for-profit organization of medical publication professionals working in the pharmaceutical, biotechnology, and device industries: http://www.ismpp.org

- **The Joint Commission.** Formerly known as the Joint Commission for the Accreditation of Hospitals (JCAH), the renamed Joint Commission remains the accrediting organization for health care organizations to ensure that patients receive high-quality care. The Joint Commission publishes standards of care that you can download online: www.jointcommission.org

- **Office of Inspector General (OIG), OIG Compliance Program Guidance for Pharmaceutical Manufacturers.** The mission of the OIG is to protect the integrity of HHS, as well as the health and welfare of the beneficiaries of those programs: http://www.oig.hhs.gov

- **US Food and Drug Administration (FDA).** The FDA is responsible for protecting the public health by assuring the safety and efficacy of human and veterinary drugs, biological products, medical devices, our nation's food supply, cosmetics, and products that emit radiation: http://www.fda.gov. For a listing of the different databases maintained by the FDA and accessible at the FDA website, go to: http://www.fda.gov/search/databases.html

Phases of Drug Development

❖ *Preclinical (animal) studies.*
Before drugs can be tested in humans, they must undergo preclinical, or animal, testing. According to the FDA, most drugs that are tested in animals never even make it to human testing and review by the FDA. Drugs that are tested successfully in animals must then go through the FDA's rigorous evaluation process, which examines everything about the drug.

❖ *Phase 1 clinical trials.*
Phase 1 studies are usually conducted in healthy volunteers, that is, people who don't have any specific disease or medical condition. The emphasis at this phase is on safety. Researchers want to learn how the drug is metabolized and excreted by the human body and whether the drug has any side effects and what they are. Phase 1 studies usually include anywhere from 20 to 80 subjects.

❖ *Phase 2 clinical trials.*
If Phase 1 trials show that a drug is not toxic, Phase 2 trials begin. At this phase, researchers focus on the drug's efficacy, that is, whether the drug works in people with a certain disease or medical condition. Some Phase 2 trials are controlled trials where patients who are receiving the study drug are compared with similar patients who are receiving a different treatment. This treatment could be a placebo (a fake drug) or a different drug. As with Phase 1 trials, investigators continue to examine safety and study short-term side effects. The number of subjects in Phase 2 trials can range from as few as 30 to as many as 300. Once Phase 2 trials are nearly complete, the FDA and the company seeking approval of the study drug determine how the Phase 3

studies will be conducted and how many patients will need to be evaluated to determine further the drug's safety and efficacy.

❖ *Phase 3 clinical trials.*

Phase 3 studies are larger clinical trials that begin once the study drug has been shown to be effective in Phase 2. In Phase 3, investigators gather more information about drug safety and efficacy, study different drug dosages, examine the drug's effects on different populations, and evaluate the study drug in combination with other drugs. Phase 3 trials can enroll several hundred people or several thousands.

❖ *Phase 4 (postmarketing) trials.*

Evaluation of drug safety and efficacy doesn't end once the FDA approves the drug for marketing. Postmarketing trials, also known as Phase 4 commitments, are studies the drug company agrees to complete after the study drug receives FDA approval. Postmarketing studies provide the FDA with additional information about a product's safety, efficacy, and optimal use.

About The Accidental Medical Writer

W hen we got started as freelance medical writers, there was very little information available to guide us and to help us avoid making mistakes. There were plenty of books on writing, and even a couple of books about freelance writing. But they were dry, not very user friendly, and definitely not very inspiring. And there was nothing written specifically to help people become freelance medical writers. With *The Accidental Medical Writer* series, we're changing all that!

This first book in our series has been created to give you the confidence you need to become a successful freelance medical writer, the motivation to take that all-important first step, and the benefit of our almost 40 years of collective experience in making it work. Armed with all that advice and insight, we realized you would then need to know how to do what we do. That's where the other books in *The Accidental Medical Writer* series come in.

We are currently working on, and have plans to soon begin, books that will show you how to write the many different types of things that freelance medical writers write: monographs, journal articles, abstracts and posters, gap analyses and publication plans, CME symposia, sales training and motivation materials, case studies, detail aids, websites, interactive media, patient education materials, videos, executive summaries, clinical study reports, investigator brochures, advisory board meetings, needs assessments, patient recruitment materials, direct mail, and medical advertising. The actual list is much longer, but you get the idea—there are a *lot* of opportunities for freelance medical writers!

The Accidental Medical Writer series will also include books to help you start, run, and grow a successful freelance medical writing business, and books to help you become the best freelance medical writer you can be. Every book in our series will be written in the same friendly,

http://www.theaccidentalmedicalwriter.com

accessible, and informative style that we hope you have found this book to be.

In developing this series, we realized that the medical writing field is continually changing and that the needs of freelance medical writers are often very immediate. This is why we've built our website— www.theaccidentalmedicalwriter.com—so we can communicate with you and help you navigate this dynamic industry, stay abreast of the latest issues, and interact with us.

At www.theaccidentalmedicalwriter.com, you'll find our answers to frequently asked questions, and be able to send us your own questions. At the website, you can read about upcoming books in *The Accidental Medical Writer* series, and sign up to be notified when new books in the series become available. From time to time, there will also be opportunities for you to participate in webinars and other continuing education programs—all designed to help you become a successful freelance medical writer.

CPSIA information can be obtained
at www.ICGtesting.com
Printed in the USA
BVHW081920221119
564529BV00002B/205/P